Roots of
Apathy

Understanding the underworld where struggling students think, feel and live.

Michael R. Hicks

Roots of Apathy

By Michael R. Hicks

Copyright

Printing February 2014

EDITED BY

Ron Hicks

Rosanne Hicks

Katie Gerbasy

PRINTED IN THE UNITED STATES BY

ISBN-13: 978-1495270048

Create Space

COVER DESIGN

Artwork (boy under tree): Brian Stanton

Layout: Ovi Dogar (www.absolutecovers.com)

<u>Acknowledgements</u>

There are many of people I would like to thank who contributed to the long and laborious process of writing this book.

First and foremost, my wife and best friend, Carmel, who gave me time and space to be a writing hermit. Thank you for all your patience and support!

Brian Stanton, who captured the essence of Roots of Apathy in the cover design. Thank you Brian for all the time you spent changing and adjusting the picture. You took an idea and created an incredible image.

Dan Hicks, my friend and brother, whose knowledge as a professional counselor helped me understand the roots of student apathy. Thank you for our many conversations and for your insights.

Ron and Rosanna Hicks, my amazing parents, who've helped so many struggling young people over the years on their ranch in Oregon. Thank you for reading through all the unedited versions of this project and for your helpful suggestions and advice.

To the hundreds of students over the years who have shared their stories. Thank you for all that you have taught me. Your experiences have helped me understand how struggling students think and feel.

On the Inside

"I know it looks like
I don't care about school.
But what you see on my outside,
is me just trying to cope
with what you don't see
on my inside.
I've got problems...
and they feel so heavy
I can't carry anything else...
not even school."

Contents

Introduction: A Book about Roots   6

Chapter 1:   Open to Page 37   10

Chapter 2:   Confession and Healing   20

Chapter 3:   Building Relational Equity   28

Chapter 4:   Facing Storms   42

Chapter 5:   My Storm is My Gift   53

Chapter 6:   Forgiveness   60

Chapter 7:   Divorce: My Family is Broken   77

Chapter 8:   The Party Train   89

Chapter 9:   Fear: It's Not Safe at My House   110

Chapter 10:   Grief: There's a Hole in My Heart   131

Chapter 11:   Lessons from Clara: Moved Again   143

Chapter 12:   Not Yet   154

Chapter 13:   Additional Stories   159

Introduction

A Book about Roots

****

I've had the distinct pleasure of being present when all four of my beautiful children were born. The first one scared the heck out of me. The rest I was prepared for. I'm struck with how much writing a book can be like a mother bringing children into the world. The "babies" grow inside for a while; sometimes a long while, but eventually they begin to make the mother uncomfortable. One day she realizes, "I've got to do this! I've got to go through the labor and get this thing out." I know I'm a guy and can't really relate, but I'm thinking that writing a book for the first time is a lot like having that first child. I wonder, will it come out right? Will it be of any interest or value? What if others have felt, and thought, the same things before me and have already written my child? I almost hesitate to do research for fear the child will somehow become illegitimate; a genetic hybrid with traits spliced in from all sorts of donors. Is that okay? Can a writer do that? Can I steal the ideas of others and then merge them with my own? I'm reminded of the ancient Jewish proverb, "There is nothing new under the sun."

I have my own version of Solomon's wisdom:

"I have never thunk a thought

That someone hasn't thunk before

And when I think I've thunk it all

Someone else will thunk of more."

As adults who work with teenagers I suspect our most useful ideas have been borne out of personal experiences and then fleshed out through many honest conversations. We share our thoughts and stories and listen to others share theirs. Along the way we grow and change. When we reflect on what we've learned over the years we become acutely aware of something profound: our best insights have already been discovered by others before us. We might think we've stumbled upon something "new", but in reality it's probably been there all along...just forgotten. I've come to believe the most effective strategies for motivating apathetic teenagers must be revisited and stirred up again from time to time. As you read

> *If to feel properly "in-serviced" you must have a lot of pedagogical jargon tossed to and fro, I suggest you pick up something else to read.*

the pages that follow you might get the distinct feeling that there's really nothing novel here, but only truth that's been lying dormant. If that be the case and *Roots of Apathy* awakens something of value from its forgotten slumber, then I will have achieved my goal. As an educator, I have been working with kids for a number of years. Both successes and failures as a teacher, coach and parent have been the hammer and anvil that have shaped the ideas in this book.

Currently, I spend half my day teaching Biology and the other half working with "at risk" students who are behind in credits and in danger of not graduating. The ideas here were born out of an effort to help those in trouble academically. What I've discovered along the way has been eye-opening and, at the same time, rejuvenating.

Over the years I have seen many intervention programs that provide academic support, but unfortunately, they often fall desperately short. Educators have a propensity to address symptoms rather than core issues. Providing homework help, for example, may not be very helpful when the home itself is broken and in chaos. Perhaps I'm stating the obvious, but apathy has roots.

This is a book about those roots!

If to feel properly "in-serviced" you must have a lot of pedagogical jargon tossed to and fro I suggest you pick up something else to read. *Roots of Apathy* is not intended to be a research-based work with lots of data and lengthy quotes from various experts in the field of education. Instead I hope you find this book an easy read; something inspirational and read for pleasure. By using original stories, penned in the vernacular of teenagers themselves, we will peer into the real, and sometimes raw world, where struggling students live. Their writings provide us with a clear perspective of what it's like to be teenagers striving to make their way through life in the midst of storms, stresses and sometimes unbearable pressures. Their stories, articulated as only teenagers can do, are powerful testimonies of how they think and feel. They help us remember our own journeys through those tumultuous years.

I also hope to stimulate some dialogue between adults; to get them talking and sharing ideas about how to understand and help the young souls who have given up on school. Some of the best ideas are not going to be included in this book. Why? Because I haven't thought of them yet…but maybe you have. As you read my insights and ideas…you'll have your own. As I share stories that kids have written, you'll recall dozens of stories from your own classroom. I hope you'll take a few ideas from these pages, add them to your own, and in the end, get better at what you already do.

So this is my progeny. I'm not sure if it's the right time or that I won't think someday that I should have waited. I suspect that before the manuscript goes to print, I'll think of something else I wish I would have written, but it will be too late. Nevertheless, I humbly offer my best insights and discoveries to the special people among us who work with the strange and wonderful creatures we call teenagers. This is a book for them; for the teachers, counselors, coaches and youth workers who have rolled up their sleeves and joined the campaign to make a difference. It's not an easy mission. The root causes that draw a student into the fog of apathy are not well understood. We can say with relative certainty however, that when we try to unravel the tangled system of roots that choke motivation, we become keenly aware of a sobering reality…it's complicated!

Chapter One

Open to Page 37

✱✱✱✱✱✱✱✱✱✱✱✱✱✱✱✱✱✱✱

It started out to be a normal day at school when yard duty took a surreal turn. From the west side of the campus, five gunshots rang out: two, followed by silence, and then three more piercing the quiet. I looked over toward P Street and saw, about a hundred yards away, a mound of clothing in the shape of a body. My first instinct was to take cover and make sense of what was happening from behind the safety of a tree trunk or building, but that was quickly interrupted by several hundred junior high kids rushing past me to reach the fence. I tried to stop them, but the energy in the air was electric and my efforts futile.

I felt like I was in a *Jurassic Park* movie and dinosaurs were stampeding past me. I realized right away I wasn't going to hold back the herd, so I became a dinosaur and joined them at the fence. Not more than thirty feet from where I parked my beat up Toyota Corolla, a boy was down in the street. I hurried over and opened a gate that led to my small parking area, secured it behind me before any students could follow, and ran to the boy.

It's hard to describe the feeling I had as I stood over the young man, who lay moaning, his eyes rolled back in their sockets. I could see a pencil-sized hole on each side of his head right about his ears. A small caliber bullet had gone straight through, and a pool of deep red blood was forming on the cold pavement under him. A colleague quickly joined me from somewhere. She knelt down, cradled the young man's head in her lap and tried to stop the blood flow with a piece of cloth while I waved away approaching cars and redirected traffic.

> *A small caliber bullet had gone straight through, and a pool of deep red blood was forming on the cold pavement under his head.*

In a matter of minutes, an ambulance, a fire truck and numerous police cars arrived on the scene. I glanced back at the schoolyard and saw dozens of students with their faces pressed against the wire fence. One girl was crying hysterically, trying desperately to get to the other side of the fence, while several friends restrained her. Apparently she knew the boy who lay wounded in the street.

Thirty minutes passed before the ambulance sped off, its siren blaring, leaving the fire department to hose down the street. I gave my statement to the police, telling them what I'd seen and heard, and was then released to return to my life as a junior high teacher. The playground by then was completely vacant, the students tucked safely away in their classrooms. Mine, however, sat empty. The choir teacher, like a mother hen, had crowded all my students into her room next door. I was grateful. I thanked her and led them all back to my own room.

Once everyone found their seats, there loomed an eerie, awkward silence as thirty five pairs of eyes stared at me, waiting for some kind of response to what had happened. I hesitated. I didn't want them to see how shaken I was. I remember swallowing hard, pretty sure if I wasn't careful I was going to cry in front of my students. So I gripped the podium with both hands, took a deep breath, steadied myself and said,

"Open your books to page 37."

Thirty-five books flew open without a word. I don't even remember what was on page 37, but I do remember the need to focus, to simply do my job.

It worked.

I made it through the next few hours, but for many days after that horrible experience, I struggled with vivid memories of the boy in the street. I kept seeing the dark, syrupy blood oozing onto the pavement, the two holes in his head and the moaning sounds he made as he struggled for life. I kept wondering who he was, this child who had been cut down. Why was he there? What had he done to deserve that kind of violence? One moment he was walking down the street, and the next he lay crumpled on the hard, cold pavement, fighting for each breath. Was he in pain? Was he afraid? Was he even aware of what had happened?

I learned later he had been a student at the alternative high school down the block. He was walking by our campus when he encountered two shooters who were waiting for him on bicycles across the street. We've all heard of drive-by shootings, but a cycle-by? Only one bullet had found its mark, but that's all it took. Three other bullets hit my building next to where I'd parked my car. One left a dent in the entrance door about two feet to the right of the doorknob at eye level. Every day, as I fumbled with my keys, I looked at that dent and remembered the gruesome events of that tragic day. Sometimes I would pause there and run my fingers through the shiny dimple that stared out toward the street like a watchful eye peering from a sniper's scope.

> *Every day, as I fumbled with my keys, I looked at that dent and remembered the gruesome events of that tragic day.*

I'll never forget that day. The images are imprinted in my mind forever and I'm a different person because of them. Although I didn't know the boy personally, I found myself grieving, though unsure why. Perhaps he represented students I did know, students I cared about, and a grim reminder that it could have been any one of them. The weeks that followed were difficult. I had to fight hard to stay focused on my work. Though one teenager had fallen, many others still poured into my room each day requiring my full attention. The memories of the dying boy had to be left outside in the street so that I could get my job done in the classroom.

Fast-forward about fifteen years: I'm teaching high school now and I'm telling that story to a group of juniors and seniors in my General Studies class. Behind in credits and in danger of not graduating, these kids are in academic trouble. The clock is ticking. If they don't get focused and make big changes soon, they won't graduate on time, perhaps not at all. Many of these are students I had as sophomores a year or two earlier in General Biology. I've seen the glaring apathy and underachievement that got them in this mess. I've even booted some of these angels out of class before. I know they can be a pain in the keister, but now we're back together and it's different this time. I feel a strange permission to be brutally honest with these students and put all the cards on the table. I'm saying things like, "Welcome to General Studies, Ladies and Girls." (That always gets a reaction.) "Can I ask you an honest question? Are you ready to turn things around? Because here's the thing; if you only do what you've always done, you'll only get what you've always got. This is your chance, perhaps your last chance. Are you ready to change?"

In preparing for these new "intervention" classes I found myself wondering, "What is the root of their apathy? How did they lose their way and get so lost?" That's when I had an epiphany; one of those special moments when something dawns on you that never has before. Actually, I had two. The first one was that maybe these kids are a lot like me! Maybe they've encountered some trauma and not known how to handle it. Maybe sometimes they feel like I did that day on yard duty. I was an adult, and a professional, and I'd found myself struggling for many days to get past the memories of that horrific shooting. At night, when I tried to sleep, I couldn't control the wave of emotions that started in my belly and swelled up through my chest. Sometimes the wave would push so hard it would leak out through my eyes. It was raw and real, a kind of grief and sadness mixed together that I couldn't explain to anyone. I covered it pretty well at school, but at home, in the quiet moments, I struggled. Repeatedly.

As I tried to help these "at risk" students, I found myself wondering, what do they struggle with in their quiet moments? When did school become unimportant to

> *Sometimes the wave would push so hard it would leak out through my eyes.*

them? What traumas are they facing that no one really understands, maybe that no one even knows about?

In short, *what are their stories?*

As an adult I was able to get control of myself that day. I gathered my thoughts, focused, and did what had to be done. I took a deep breath and grabbed the podium. I steadied myself and said, "Open your books to page 37." But maybe these kids can't do that yet, maybe they don't know how. Most kids aren't mature enough, or strong enough, to stay in control through difficult circumstances. Most of them are not able to put aside the traumas in their lives and stay focused on what needs to be done. For the confused and struggling students in our classrooms, that kind of strength and resilience may not have been modeled at home.

So, on that first day of General Studies class, I told them the story of my youth, how things got rough at my home when I was their age. I told them about the rebellious six months during my sophomore year when I dabbled in drugs, got high, punched a kid in shop class, and mastered the art of lying. I shared how my parents went through some ugly times as they struggled to hold their marriage together, and how confused and traumatized I was during those episodes. I opened up and made myself vulnerable to them. I let them know I was no stranger to storms or to the

> *Apathy is the outward fruit we see, but the roots are something else, something deeper and more elusive.*

reality that sometimes school doesn't seem very important when a dark cloud of anger, pain, fear and hurt enshroud everything.

Then, I asked them to tell me their story. We began with "Family and School History." Starting with first grade, they recorded notes about every one of their years in school, their favorite teachers, favorite subjects, and memories good and bad. I asked them to share details about when it was that they first began to lose interest in school and I asked if they knew what had caused the change.

Some of the students were understandably guarded and kept to the facts. Others opened up and wrote page, after page, after page. Their stories were incredible! There was abuse, divorce, adoption, fathers or mothers who were soldiers deployed in Iraq, drugs, bad friends, juvenile hall, fighting, expulsions, complete lack of supervision and dysfunctional parents, just to mention a few. Some students had attended as many as ten different schools in eleven years. One young man said his parents were "back East somewhere" and he hadn't seen them in years. I asked how he had gotten to the West Coast and he said he and his brother came out by train.

"Amtrak?"

"No. Boxcars."

I'd hitchhiked home from college a few times, against my parents' wishes, but teenagers traveling cross-country in boxcars rendered me momentarily speechless.

Reading their stories has done me much good. I think I'm beginning to understand the source of their all too familiar I don't care attitude. Apathy is the outward fruit that we see, but the roots are something deeper and more elusive. Underneath the surface are the real culprits: anger, discouragement, depression, fear, hurt and loneliness. Add to that a tablespoon of shame, a cup of regret and a half-gallon of hopelessness and you have the makings of a pretty healthy pot of apathy. Some students have failed for so long that they can no longer see themselves as ever being successful. They've "screwed up" too much and now they believe those fleeting opportunities for success have slipped through their fingers, never to be realized. Resigned to their lot, they fall into the pit of apathy and concede: "What the hell? Why even try?"

In many of their stories I see a familiar pattern. Things started out pretty normal in school until the dark cloud of trauma swept in and devastation followed. Some of their problems stem from their own inability to make good choices when bad friends offered them a refuge. We all know about that—the powerful pull to belong and fit in, no matter what the cost. In other cases, it was simply an unfortunate series of one raw deal after another. Life's circumstances were literally out of their

> *Our frustration and impatience with these kids is understandable, but it won't help them find their way out of the dark cloud of apathy.*

control. Bounced around like yo-yos, by parents ill-equipped to deal with their own problems, these kids suffered privately. But, when they got old enough, they rebelled. Usually not so quietly— or so privately.

I have found myself oddly energized by this new, challenging assignment. I look in the faces of these young people and I see a light in their eyes. Some of them are working harder than they've worked since the dark cloud arrived. They'll probably screw up again a time or two before it's all said and done, but I'm ready for that. I did too.

Here's the second epiphany I had: I'm seeing that if I take a risk and get a little vulnerable, even share some of my own story, these struggling students might glimpse some hope from my success. I too lost my way for a stretch of my life, but found it again, and maybe pieces of my story can encourage them to give school another try. Let's be honest. Many of us screwed up when we were younger, but we turned out all right. If students knew that the adults in their lives could actually relate to their struggles, that we can understand the distractions of a dysfunctional family or the temptations of unhealthy friendships, they might be willing to take a risk and make a connection. They might reach back and meet us in the middle somewhere. They might even put aside their traumas for a moment and find the strength to cope a little better with their private struggles. Maybe, with some support, they might even take a deep breath, steady themselves and start doing what needs to be done.

Our frustration and impatience with these kids is understandable, but it won't help them find their way out of the dark cloud of apathy. What many of them need is love, support, understanding and a reason to hope. Now, I know that teachers and counselors and those of us who work with kids didn't exactly sign up for that. God knows we'd rather strangle the little rebels sometimes, but for many of them, we may be their last chance. I'm not saying we are able to personally save them all. Some of my students may not be reachable at this moment, at least not by me, but they may be the very students that only *you* can reach. Your story might be just the story they need to hear that gives them hope and a reason to try. And if you've traveled by boxcar across the country at age fourteen, call me. I'll hook you up with this kid I know.

So, here's what I'm saying: tell a little of your story to your students—and listen to a little of theirs. Sometimes that's all it takes to break through to kids who otherwise see you as just another adult enemy in their lives.

I'm finding that a strange thing happens when you discover the roots of students' apathy. It draws you in. You feel more connected. With all the traumas hidden in their lives, you realize something profound. The most important thing you may ever teach them is how to take a deep breath, steady themselves, and open their books to page 37.

Chapter Two

Confession and Healing

****

"How do I feel about this assignment? It actually seems like a good idea, for everybody I think, whether they know it or not. Writing your life story gets you thinking and starts you putting your thoughts to paper. In life, everybody has problems, everybody has trouble, but, at times, it can just be too much for someone to handle. And, when you share your story, when you tell a friend or even a complete stranger about something that has made you sad, or something horrible, it makes the burden of carrying it seem just that little bit lighter. It's like having a friend help you get a heavy load off your back. I always feel better about my problems after talking to a friend about them. That's why I think this assignment is a very good idea. Not everybody has a friend they can go to when something really hard is going on in their life."

Apathy usually has roots that we don't see. The roots are hidden and often carefully guarded. After all, even in the adult world, no one wants their dark secrets exposed. The problem is baggage gets very heavy, very fast. The strain of carrying it around wears people down. Although they are exhausted, they don't know how to unburden themselves. Sometimes they start believing that their baggage defines who they are—it becomes their identity.

Young people are no different. Those we see struggling in school are often dragging a huge bundle of hidden traumas and pent-up emotions. Imagine a fishnet full of fear, anger, shame, regret, confusion, depression and loneliness. Parents are divorcing, Grandpa is dying, unhealthy friends are beckoning—the list goes on. The roots are varied, but they often grow into a deep, tangled mess that becomes quite cumbersome. This net of stress-producing circumstances can get hung up at every turn and, consequently, forward progress, personal growth and academic achievement may come to a screeching halt. So how can we help those who feel defeated by their burdens empty that net? How can we help weary students regain a measure of freedom and get them moving, growing and achieving once again?

> *A strange thing seems to happen when the net breaks open. Healing!*

A great place to start is simply getting them to tell their story. You might be wondering, "How in the world are we going to get low-achieving teenagers to be honest about their hidden struggles? Do they even have the capacity to recognize them?" I'll admit it's not as easy as it sounds. It requires that they trust us.

Their secrets must be kept safe and we must never expose them or judge them. So, how do we get them to trust us enough to open up?

A powerful beginning can be sharing pieces of our own story. If we open the door and let them see that we have baggage of our own, that we've struggled and been hindered in our progress as well, they may begin to trust us with their story. They might even start believing us when we say we understand.

Keep in mind that, if we want to build trust, we have to listen without judgment, and even when their youthful logic is flawed and misguided, we need to be patient. We must let them tell their story as *they* perceive it.

There is a well-known 17th century Scottish proverb that says, "Confession is good for the soul." It really is. A strange thing happens when the net breaks open—healing!

"Ah, someone knows; someone understands; someone finally gets me."

Of course, it's not complete healing, but with every measure of disclosure, received without judgment or rejection, comes an ever-increasing glimmer of hope. With hope comes light. You can actually see it in their eyes. Their countenance brightens. When the light starts to come back, the dark cloud of apathy begins to fade. The talons of past failures lose their grip and the net of trauma and emotion becomes less of a burden. In time they may feel able to cast the net aside completely.

Freedom!

We can't expect low-achieving, at-risk students, to make academic success their priority. They're too busy dragging their problems around. So why don't we begin right there? Why don't we help them deal with the fishnet first? Why not give them a chance to understand the roots beneath their own apathy and help them heal a little before we press them to become achievers?

While enormously helpful, for some, writing their school and family history is a very difficult thing to do. They often stare blankly into space because they honestly don't know where to begin. They're not certain if they should—or even could—share some of the dark chapters of their lives. A little priming of the pump might be necessary. Once the pencil gets moving, however, the stories tend to flood out across the paper all by themselves. I am always amazed at how quiet the room gets when 40 students are writing their school and family histories. Some of the lowest-achieving students have shocked me with some of the most beautifully articulated autobiographies. I don't cry easily, but I've choked up while reading more than a few of them.

Other stories are just enjoyable to read because teenagers have such a unique way of expressing themselves. Below is a story that had me smiling from the first line. By the end, I understood how the downward spiral in school came about. It made perfect sense. If only her teachers had known her story, they might have been a little softer and a little more patient. The first part she wrote at the beginning of her senior year, when she first entered my class.

In first grade, my teacher had a gigantic praying mantis as a class pet. I swear the thing was at least seven inches long. It fascinated me.

In second grade I remember that I got yelled at by a teacher for the first time. It was because this girl had taken all the markers. I asked her to give me some and she pushed me, so I tackled her. The teacher scared me to death. I moved to California from Canada in second grade. This was a huge change for me and I had the most horrible teacher. She reminded me of a witch. She had these horrible, long fingernails and when she'd get mad she'd scream and come at you with her nasty nails. She scarred me for life.

The only thing I remember about third grade was that we had kindergarten buddies. They would come into our class and we had to read short stories to them. My buddy was really strange. He would just sit there and, if anyone approached him, he would growl at them and snap his teeth. I think he might have been in one of his animal phases.

Fourth grade I had the best teacher I've ever had. He was awesome because he taught in a way that made me understand school and I actually wanted to get up to go to school in the morning. I was on the honor roll all year with him with straight A's. I had the same teacher again for fifth grade and I made the honor roll with straight A's all year again.

In the sixth grade, I lost my grandfather—he and I were really close—and one of my closest friends also died that same week. It was in the beginning of school so it really affected me. I was never able to recover my grades that year and my teachers didn't understand. I was labeled as a "problem child" the rest of that year. I started to believe it myself and fell into a routine of not doing my homework, doing badly on tests and just not giving a rat's ass about school. I got in a lot of fights and just didn't have any respect for myself, either. I felt myself sinking into a depression, but I didn't want people to know. I didn't think they'd care.

Grief. Sadness. Confusion! This little girl lost her way when death hit close to home. Her world got rocked and in that difficult season she lost her grip on school. The honor student fell behind. The sweet, smart child became apathetic and difficult. Somehow her teachers missed it. They didn't understand.

Her story went on to tell of more struggles throughout her middle and high school years and of conflicts at home with her parents. Over time, she developed a tough, protective exterior. She made it clear that she wasn't about to soften for anyone, especially not for another adult who only pretended to care.

> *I felt myself sinking into a depression, but I didn't want people to know.*

I've seen this disposition before with other students, especially when I ask them to write their stories. They can get pretty brash. It's as if they want to establish the ground rules right away.

"OK, you want to know my story? Well here it is: I don't trust adults. And guess what? You're an adult, so get lost!" The "in your face" attitude pushes many of us who want to help away. Most struggling students don't respond all warm and fuzzy when we offer a helping hand. We care and reach out— and they snarl and bite back. So, what do we typically do? We back off and leave them alone to navigate tidal waves of grief and confusion alone.

These kids need us to care about them. *Relentlessly!* They only soften with time and lots of patience.

Now you might be thinking, "Time and patience? Who has that to give? We're teachers. We're busy. We have 200 other learners to deal with, so the really prickly ones will have to fend for themselves." Right?

I don't think so. The prickly ones need us the most. In fact, they may be the ones with whom we can make the biggest difference.

At the end of the school year, I ask my students to write the next chapter of their school history, the chapter that included the year we had just completed. I was touched by what this same tough girl wrote. It took ten months, but the hardened shell had softened. What was hidden underneath was a pretty amazing kid.

I started senior year expecting it to be like all the other years, with uncaring teachers and stupid students that don't care. But then I got put in a General Studies class. First of all, I did not like the teacher. I was suspicious of him. No teacher had ever tried to get under my skin before, to try and see who I was under my tough exterior. I didn't like it one bit. It made me nervous. But then I realized that he wasn't doing it to hurt me or to use it against me. He truly cared about what I had to say. I started to think that maybe letting people see who I really am isn't all that bad. I started to believe in myself as well. I started trying in school again and now I'm graduating with better grades than I've had in years. It made my senior year fun and I learned so much about myself. I know now that I can do well in the world and that it's not just a place full of uncaring people. I'm going to college in the fall. I have a good job and my life is going somewhere. My senior year has been the best ever!

Telling our stories and listening to others tell theirs can cause a kind of "open confession" that can lead to a special kind of healing. I didn't expect that.

When you encounter difficult students, those who seem troubled, make a conscious effort to ask them about their lives. If they don't feel safe telling you their whole story at first, be patient and just keep caring. Some days you'll have to give them space; other days you'll need the patience of a saint. But just keep gently prodding, caring and listening. Let every day with them be a new day. Push yesterday's shortcomings to the forgotten fringe. Keep short accounts of past conflicts and let today's encounter with them be fresh and new.

Always remember: beneath the hard exterior there are amazing human beings; young people with all the hopes, dreams and aspirations that you and I also had when we were that age. They might be a little broken and damaged when they get to us, perhaps a little hard to reach, so when it comes to caring, pack your lunch. Having a lasting impact takes a while.

Care relentlessly! They're worth it.

Chapter Three

Building Relational Equity

****

Believe it or not, most teenagers think adults are clueless. We don't get them. For them to acknowledge that we might actually be right about something is suicide. For many teens, it's much worse to admit that adults are right than to be outrageously wrong.

"Surrender? Are you kidding? Never!"

Before we become too hard on these little rebels, we should be honest with ourselves. Even we adults aren't convinced that other adults fully understand us. Unless they have truly walked in our shoes, we aren't willing to accept that they could possibly know how we feel. People who don't move in the circles we move in don't always understand. They miss the subtle nuances. They don't know the code and as a result, trust is given cautiously.

When it comes to trust, there is a natural chasm between teens and the adults in their lives. We don't get them and, as a result, we become yet another frustrated adult in their lives. We nag, scold and admonish them for their poor effort, subpar attendance and lack of attention to their education. We confront them, and they snap back at us. We press them, and they react with defiance and disrespect. We try to reason with them, (code for *lecture*), and they become argumentative.

Some don't act out openly, but instead keep their heads down and concede in silence. Rather than focusing their hostility on us, they turn it inward. "I'm such a disappointment, such a failure." Our frustration with them reinforces what they already believe about themselves – they don't measure up. It looks like apathy to us, but, behind the veil, it's actually a combination of depression and discouragement. From within the dark cloud of hopelessness, a voice whispers: "You're broken. You won't get fixed. You've fallen and you'll never really recover. You are not special or significant. You're unattractive and worthless." Peering out of the cloud they see us standing there, frustrated, and they conclude, "They don't understand. They don't get me... and they never will."

Consider this: to reach them we must intentionally build *"Relational Equity."*

I had never heard that expression used before, but one day I was trying to explain the concept of building connections with students and it came to me. It's like a bank deposit. The more we put into the account, the more we can draw out. Relational equity comes from deposits we make into a person's life. The value accrues – not all at once, but slowly.

Sometimes an opportunity will present itself to make a large deposit all at once, but most come in small amounts over an extended period of time. A dime here (a compliment), a quarter there (a word of affirmation), and the piggy bank of relational equity begins to fill.

When the big deposit opportunities do come along, they usually require an extraordinary extension of ourselves into the life of a teenager. When those moments present themselves they remind us that the best part of being an educator has very little to do with teaching Biology, or Math or English. It's those unexpected situations that often provide the most significant human connections. Those encounters are what make teaching so rewarding.

One of those moments came on a day when one of my students appeared down and discouraged. I asked her, "What's wrong?" Her eyes filled with tears. She answered, "Don't ask, Hicks." I could tell she was afraid she might break down in front of the other

> *I had no answers, or profound words of wisdom for her, only two big empathetic ears.*

students, so I asked if she'd like to talk about it later and she nodded. After class, when the others had gone to lunch, she shared her troubles. It was supposed to be a good day – her birthday – but instead it had become a day of pain and heartache. Hurtful words from an older brother had led to an explosive verbal fight. His words cut deep when he reminded her that she was not a real member of the family – she was only adopted. That pressed painfully on a deeply buried wound and soon the yelling broke into an all-out physical altercation. Punches were thrown, knuckles and arms got bruised, and a vase was broken over the brother's head. In the end, the police were called.

I had no answers, or profound words of wisdom for her, only two, big, empathetic ears. After finishing her story, and shedding a few more tears, she thanked me for listening and headed out to find some lunch.

Later that day, while thinking about this young lady, an idea came to me. I recalled the story she had written for me earlier in the year where she described how her mother had given birth to her in Mexico while her father was away. A few weeks later she was brought to California and left with relatives. Abandoned by her parents, she grew up without knowing her father or hearing him say those important words of affirmation, praise and encouragement that kids so desperately need to hear. It occurred to me that maybe I could pinch-hit for her dad on this, her eighteenth birthday, and write her a card.

You had a birthday this week and it should have been a special day. But instead of being a time to celebrate and be happy, it turned out to be a week with a lot of heartache and hurt feelings. I'm so sorry it went like that.

Life seems to give us a lot of unexpected difficulties sometimes and you have certainly had your share. You actually have a lot in common with my mom. She never knew her father or her mother. For reasons she never fully understood, they gave her up for adoption at birth. And, although a new family stepped up and took her in as their own, she always had questions and deep feelings about it all. She wondered "Why me? Why did all this have to happen?"

I've been thinking about your situation and I have a hunch there are some things you have missed out on growing up, things that every daughter needs, things that every daughter should hear their father say. I have two daughters of my own and, if you were my third, you would have known how special you are from the time you were just a child.

If you were my daughter growing up I would have tucked you in at night and would have said to you a thousand times over:

"I am so proud of you!"

"You are an amazing daughter."

"You are so smart and capable."

"You can do anything you put your mind to."

"You are so beautiful!"

I would have told you:

"You are so talented!"

"You have such a great future ahead of you."

"You will be an amazing mom one day."

"Always remember, your father loves you very much!"

I would have prayed:

"Dear God, protect my little girl. Keep her safe. Bring the right young man into her life and help her wait patiently for him. Dear God, let her know how much You love her. And God, thank you for such a wonderful daughter."

Those are things we all need to hear, so this week, the week of your eighteenth birthday, I wanted you to hear them. Why?

Because they are all true. I see it in you. You are an incredible young lady. You've become so strong and beautiful, even though you didn't get handed a perfect life.

God has His hand on you young lady, and He has special things in store for your future.. Don't get discouraged, just keep moving forward through these storms and never, ever give up. You're amazing!

Mr. Hicks

There is a special kind of blessing that is supposed to get passed on from fathers and mothers to sons and daughters. It's a blessing that rides on the back of things spoken; like praise, affirmation, and simple words that communicate love. Too many of our students don't hear those spoken words at home and it leaves them insecure and unsure of themselves. It's hard for them to feel worthy and valuable if they don't hear that message from those closest to them. Maybe hearing those words spoken, even from us, can make a difference.

I left the card on the little couch in the front of my room near my desk. It's where my TAs (teacher's assistants) often sit. I was busy with other duties when she found and read the card, but when I finally sat down at my desk, I looked over at her and she said, "Mr. Hicks, you made me tear up." That was all. But it was enough.

Connection. Deposit. Relational Equity!

You might wonder, "Did it make any difference for her in school? Was it all just nice feelings and warm fuzzies, or was there progress and change academically?" For this young lady the data speaks volumes. Her freshman and sophomore years she had a .66 and a .83 grade point average, but after entering the General Studies class her grades jumped to a 3.0 both her junior and senior years. With some additional online courses, and some hard work, she got her credits caught up and one warm evening in May, dressed in a red robe, she sat with her classmates on the football field waiting. Finally her name was called and she walked across the stage, shook the Principal's hand and received her high school diploma.

For those who work with teenagers, every day is full of opportunities to build relational equity. It can be a simple word of affirmation, an expression of genuine concern or an unexpected action that can make a huge difference.

Here are some other examples:

Pick up the phone and call a parent to tell him how amazing their child is and how proud you are of their efforts in your class (even if you see just a glimmer of effort, or morsel of improvement). Bear in mind, a good report from school can help a student immensely when there is conflict at home.

One afternoon I made a call like that. I knew things were rocky at home for one of my students. She felt like she could never make her dad happy. The next day she walked into my classroom and blurted out, "Mr. Hicks, you freaked me out!"

"What do you mean?" I said.

"You called my house. When I got home, my dad said, 'Your teacher called.' Dude, I was so scared. Then he told me you said I was doing great in your class." she beamed. "I was so worried."

No more was said, but I could see the grin on her face and the uncharacteristic gleam in her eye. That phone call made life a little easier for her at home. It only cost me a few minutes of my time, but it was a big deposit in our relationship. The smile alone was worth it.

Some parents simply don't believe their kids when they say things are good at school, and, in many cases, their mistrust is understandable. For the students in my General Studies classes, I used to collect weekly progress reports from all their teachers. I poured over them carefully to see where they needed help or accountability. One day, I praised a student for an unusually good report from two teachers who had noted his improved attitude and effort. I decided a quick text to both parents' cell phones might be warranted. I wrote: *"This is Mr. Hicks, your son's General Studies teacher. Wanted to let u know he has 3 A's and 1 B on his progress report. 2 teachers commented on how well he is doing. He is low on his Chemistry grade so that's a place to focus, but overall great job this quarter so far.*

His mother texted back, *"Fantastic. Thanks for letting me know."*

His father, rather than sending me a text message, called me. Apparently, their son had a history of pulling the wool over their eyes when it came to weekly progress reports, so he was suspicious. They had already caught him forging teacher signatures and now he thought his son had elevated his game to fabricating positive reports via text messages. Mom was perhaps the gullible one, but Dad needed verification. Good for him. Too many parents don't double-check and verify what their little angels are telling them. This time everybody was happy. The student had actually earned praise the honest way, through hard work and a good attitude. In the process, he earned back some trust with his parents. Me, I made a huge deposit in our relationship – equity! I might need to draw from that equity later in the semester if his grades began to dip. If that happened, the gloves may need to come off, and another, not-so-glowing text to his parents, might be in order. Here are some other ideas:

- Choose a student for an award, even if you have to make one up.
- Work with a counselor to discreetly help a student living in poverty get some new clothes or a makeover at a salon. (Powerful)
- Help a student get a job.
- When possible, and appropriate, share a personal story to show how you struggled through storms when you were younger. (Credibility)
- Allow a student to journey with you through grief, illness, or trouble in your own family. They will come to feel like family. (Connection made)
- When appropriate, do a home visit or visit a student or their family member in the hospital.

These are just a few examples. Big deposits are often things you cannot plan in advance – they come up unexpectedly. When they do, and if you're paying attention, you will recognize them as opportune moments, ones that could make a big difference in a struggling student's life. Those are the moments that transcend teaching the curriculum and usher us into the realm of just being people: some with needs, and others who care. Watch for those moments.

More typical are the small deposits. Making them can become as common as tying our shoes. Keep in mind that many teenagers who struggle in school are not accustomed to hearing compliments and words of affirmation. When they do it can have a powerful impact.

- Nice work there.
- Nice diagram. You've got skills. Ever think of becoming an art major?
- Great game last night. You were amazing!
- Nice shoes. Where did you get them?
- Thanks for helping your partner. You'll make a good employee one day. I'd hire you!
- You really stayed focused today. Good job!
- The silent fist bump with a nod and an approving smile, (subtle, unimposing) This works well with the student too cool to handle a straight-on compliment in front of peers. Academic achievement may be synonymous with "nerd", so keep the praise on the "down low."
- Empathize. Affirm and acknowledge how difficult a situation might be. "It must be hard getting your

homework done with your mom in the hospital. How can I help? Do you need a little more time?"

One of my favorite relational equity builders is eating in the cafeteria with students a few times a week. It's a powerful way to connect. I often find it more interesting than eating in the faculty dining area (no offense to my colleagues). I love to walk up to a kid I don't know and ask, "Are you gonna eat that?" At first they look at me like I'm insane. "Uh…yeah." I put on a disappointed puppy face, and then grin and walk away. Have a sense of humor. Be a little unpredictable. Students are more cooperative *in* the classroom when you've first had some positive and enjoyable contact with them *outside* of class.

You can probably think of a hundred more ways to make deposits and build equity with your own students. It only requires being on the lookout for ways to praise, encourage, connect and support. Some of you might say:

"I didn't sign up for that. I'm a teacher, not a counselor."

"I'm supposed to be an authority figure. I'm an adult, not a buddy."

"I don't have time to get sentimental. School is business. I'm the boss and the students are my employees. If they don't want to take it seriously, they will face the consequences."

"They made their beds; they can sleep in them."

Do you hear yourself in any of these comments? Do you keep a safe, professional distance from your students? Keep in mind that distance prevents connection, and connection is a powerful key to unlocking the potential in a difficult student. We have all crossed paths with a few teachers who really don't seem to like kids very much. They may love their content, but children drive them crazy. I've known a few like that. Like the teacher who declared in frustration, "I had a great lesson planned, but then the students showed up and spoiled it." Young people can spot those kind of teachers three halls away. Unfortunately, not all educators aspire to be the kind of teacher they would want for their own child. So, why should we make the effort to connect and build relational equity? Because touching the hearts of kids is our business, and the day will come when we are going to need to make a withdrawal.

> *Students are more cooperative in class when you've had positive contact with them outside of class.*

Connecting on a deeper, more personal level, builds the foundation from which accountability and straight talk about responsible behavior can take place. Sooner or later, we will have to confront the apathy that has become the pattern of behavior for these students. We can't be naive. These are the knuckleheads, the difficult ones who regularly miss school, who haven't put much effort into their education. Even if they like us, they aren't going to change overnight. They will have their moments and we will have ours. Some days they will be wearing cleats and jumping up and down on our last nerve. Let's face it: failing students are difficult to help. They need large doses of tough love, but, as adults, we have a propensity to get tough before we've been loving.

Love first!

Let that sink in a minute. Being tough with difficult students won't achieve very much if you don't *love first*! Connect as much as possible through deposits, big and small. And, when the battle lines get drawn on a difficult day, it won't be a game breaker. Most challenges can be met with a simple comment like, "Come on, Joey. Work with me! You know I like you, but you're making my job really hard today." Or, "Why are you being so difficult today, Sarah? You should know I'm not afraid to go back to prison." Then smile and move on.

Most confrontations can be handled with little fanfare if we avoid forcing a showdown. Even some of the most challenging students will cooperate if we give them a little space, especially if they know we care about them. In truth, they really don't want to lose that special connection we have built with them. They've shared their stories with us and we didn't judge them. They got a little transparent with us about the roots of their apathy and we didn't reject them. We've encouraged them, given them praise, told them we see greatness in them and believed in them. We may be one of the few adults in this world that they actually like, who actually "gets them". That's a powerful thing.

It's equity!

It will carry us through the strain and difficulty of helping them recognize, and possibly change, their destructive patterns. When they get a little ugly with us, we'll be more patient. And, when we have to get a little ugly with them, by setting boundaries, giving consequences or holding them accountable, they will be more willing to listen to our perspective, consider our counsel, and even lay down their pride to comply with our demands.

The truth is that not only have we come to care about *them*, but they have come to care about *us* as well. When we have taken the time and made the effort to build relational equity, our approval becomes important to them. It has value, even to the hardest kid with the deepest roots. When we have built equity in a relationship, we may become the very person who can help them heal their heart, lift their head, and eventually change.

What a responsibility. What an honor! Having positive, *lasting impact* on a young life; it doesn't get any better than that!

Chapter Four

Facing Storms

****

I've been involved in the sport of wrestling most of my life. It began in my elementary years with kid programs and being around my dad's high school team. As I got older and began to compete in junior high, high school and five years of college, I got pretty thick-skinned when it came to injuries. I broke my nose, separated my shoulder three times, strained a lot of ligaments and ran into a finger that lacerated my eye ball and left a scar. It was not until I was coaching in my late forties that my trusty left knee began to give me fits. It started with a popping sound that scared the be-geezers out of me, but didn't really hurt that much. It felt like a miniature dislocation. Fortunately, it always faithfully popped back into place. By age fifty, the popping sensation became more frequent, and though it still snapped back to where it belonged, it hurt like crazy. Of course all true athletes glory in their wounds and scars – it displays their toughness and prowess in their chosen craft.

One night, while sitting on the side of my bed, I explained to my wife the particulars of this progressing disability. "Check this out honey," I said. "Every time I move my leg into this certain position, it snaps out and hurts like—." Well, as if on cue, my trusty knee joint gave way at that very instant and, screaming like a girl, I thrashed about on the bed until it snapped back into place. Of course, my wife finds moments like these quite amusing.

Not too long after that episode, I was preparing to watch Brett Favre on Monday Night Football, and like I often do, I tucked my left foot under my buttocks and plopped down on the couch in my favorite half-yoga position. My knee immediately popped. The pain was excruciating. This time, however, there was no snapping back into place. My leg was stuck at a 45-degree angle and no amount of thrashing about could get it back where it belonged. This was trouble with a capital "T." It took two, very uncomfortable days, before I could see a surgeon and go under the knife.

When we can't make something difficult go away, we try to endure it.

What an amazing thing outpatient surgery is. A little poke in the arm for the I.V. and then the countdown, 10, 9, 8... and it was over. One minute I was counting backwards and the next I was waking up in the recovery room. A simple arthroscopic procedure had removed a piece of renegade cartilage and I was good as new. In times like these that I wonder what life was like before anesthesia. How did people survive surgeries without the I.V. and the countdown?

I can't imagine during the Civil War having a bullet dug out of my stomach or having my leg amputated, all without anesthesia. How does a person get through something like that? It is sometimes claimed that the phrase "bite the bullet" actually refers to a practice used by soldiers several hundred years ago to help them endure the pain of field surgery. It has become a metaphor used for bracing oneself against intense pain or discomfort. In many ways, biting the bullet is still a common practice today when people are faced with uncontrollable hardship of one kind or another. When we can't make something difficult go away, we try to endure it. When storms come along in life, we grit our teeth, hunker down and hold on by our fingernails until they blow over – if they ever do. We employ endurance to get us through the discomfort, and though helpful, it is not a very proactive response to hardship. Perseverance, on the other hand, is a very different response.

After a little study of the Greek etymology, I discovered that perseverance and endurance are not quite the same thing. When people persevere they don't hunker down; instead, they advance and move forward *in the face of a storm.* Perseverance, unlike endurance, is not a static response; it doesn't sit still. When people persevere they deliberately move forward against opposition or difficulty in their life.

What a concept!

I shared this idea with my students one day and we talked about the storms they had encountered in their lives. For some, it was an alcoholic parent, an unhealthy friendship or the heartache of a broken family. For others, it was the loss of a beloved family member, suffering through the chaos of a dysfunctional family or surviving abuse of one kind or another. Students may be living through a lot of different kinds of "storms," but the effects can often be very similar. The storms pound them and knock them off their feet. They get hammered with the rain of fear, the sleet of discouragement and the cold snow of hopelessness. What do they do to survive? Most just try to endure. They hunker down to wait it out, hoping that someday it will get better. Maybe their parents will get back together. Maybe, with time, the ache of losing someone loved will go away. Once they're eighteen, maybe they can just leave and move away from all the confusion and chaos at home. Struggling young people survive by enduring, but they don't usually know how to persevere. They don't know how to stand up and face the wind. They don't have the strength or self-discipline to lean forward and advance directly into the face of a storm. That's where we come in.

Moving forward under stormy circumstances is not easy. They may prefer calm, sunny days, but struggling young people don't usually control the weather conditions of their lives. That's why they must learn to persevere if they are going to succeed. They have to learn to swim upstream against the sometimes relentless opposing current. Endurance alone is not enough to prevent them from being swept away. If they want to achieve significantly in school, as well as in life, they must get those arms working and swim. They must kick and paddle their way forward against the tide of discouragement and despair.

What can a teacher, counselor or youth worker do to help?

For starters, we can help them set small goals and give them the support they need to advance…even if only to the nearest rock. Once they cling to that first anchor, they can hold on for a moment to catch their breath and enjoy their success. When they're ready, we can help them set a new goal, to shove off and swim even further upstream. Identifying small achievable targets is vital to helping a student who has given up on school. Looking too far ahead can be overwhelming, so we focus on something closer, something doable today.

Perseverance is an active response to hardship, but it requires courage, resilience, and sometimes, extraordinary determination. Just discussing with my classes about the difference between perseverance and endurance inspired some of my students. I saw the light flicker on as they got a picture of what they needed to do. They seemed to understand they had been hunkering down too long and it was time to get up and advance!

Students who are plagued by apathy and low achievement in our schools today are not some strange anomaly; they are everywhere we look. Educators, counselors and parents alike get frustrated as we try to understand and help them. What we often forget is that the strength and resilience they do have is often spent simply trying to endure the storms. There's not much energy left for perseverance. Some of them are hanging on by a thread, trying to get through the problems of the day. Just putting one foot in front of the other requires all their strength and it's exhausting. In their minds, effort expended on non-essentials is not imperative; it will have to wait. Unfortunately, school often becomes one of those non-essentials. In fact, poor achievement in school, and the consequences that follow, can become one more swirling gust of wind in an already overwhelming hurricane of stress. Some students just give up, check out and stop coming to school altogether.

After talking in class about the difference between perseverance and endurance, my students and I settled on a working definition.

Perseverance:

Advancing in character in the face of a storm.

I asked my students to write a description of a storm in their life and how this definition of perseverance might apply. I love the way kids think. They have a way of saying the most profound things in such simple language. Here's what one of them wrote:

"Sometimes you reach a point in your life that seems unbearable. Sometimes you think that you can't survive it. Sometimes it feels like all you can do is sit and wait for it to pass. Well, when you just sit there, it can just make it worse. Sometimes you need to fight back against this problem or try to keep going and not let it slow you down. I know. I've had some tough times. Sometimes they make you want to stop and feel bad for yourself. I've noticed that you can't do that. You have things to do. When you just stop, then more problems start to build up. Soon enough you can't get yourself out of the big hole you made that started as

a simple ditch. So when life gives you something horrible, just push through it.

This young man hit the nail on the head. When students don't fight their way forward, they fall further behind. Apathy causes their problems to snowball. Young people actually get that – they just don't always have the knowledge or the willpower to advance against the storms on their own. They've not seen perseverance modeled. What they really need is to learn how to do more than tread water. They need to learn to swim.

I know a few parents who believe the best way to teach a child to swim is to drag them, kicking and screaming in terror to the edge of the water, and throw them in. They'll figure it out, or drown trying. Well, I've met some pretty amazing kids who've learned perseverance through a similar method. They found the courage to face their fears and make a move forward all on their own.

For the first fourteen years of my short life I had to watch my dad drink every day. Maybe you think that this is no big deal, but my dad didn't stop there. My dad would get violent with anything that got in his way; including me and my family. Every day for fourteen years all I could do was go to my room, lock the door and hear my dad beat my mom. My mom would scream and cry and after my dad was done taking out his anger on her, she would still find the strength to ignore everything that just happened and come tuck me into bed. One day I had had enough. I remember walking out of my room and seeing my dad beat my mom but this time I stepped up. I looked my dad in the eye and said, "Is this the type of man you really want to be?" I could see the look of disappointment in his eyes for a minute, and then he quickly turned and started beating me.

Even though I knew my dad was an alcoholic, I figured it was time to step up and be a man, the man my dad never was. So, the next morning when I got up, I invited my dad to sit on the couch with me and I asked him, "Are you happy being the man you are?" He stayed quiet for a century, so it seemed, but then he looked me in the eye, held his chin up high and for the first time in years gave me a hug. He said, "No son, I'm not."   From that day on he started changing a little at a time and today my dad has been sober for about three years.

So you see, if you're going through a struggle like I went through, it's time for you to "come out of your room," look at your struggle in the eye and fight against the storm.

I admire kids like this young man. I can see his face right now while I share his story. It chokes me up. I wish you could know him too and could see his gentle disposition. He did drop the ball and got himself behind in school his freshman and sophomore years. He became discouraged and lost hope for a while, but the next year he turned things around. With some encouragement and support he ended his junior year with a 2.7 GPA. He's a fighter. He scratched and clawed his way forward and today he's on a better path. He's advancing in the face of his storms...that's perseverance.

His senior year, he came and shared his story with my sophomore class. He has a powerful testimony and message of hope. As adults, we can help a struggling young person see the difference between simply enduring and fighting their way forward. We can say the words they so desperately need to hear.

"Come on, get up. You can make it."

"Fight!"

We can ask them, "What do you think you need in order to move forward?" Then we can help them explore their options and set some reachable goals. We can guide them as they carefully draw up a realistic plan and then help them find the tools they need to make it happen. We can also share with them the stories of others who persevered before them. Maybe a piece of our own story will give them hope. One student concluded his "Life Story" assignment with the following sentence:

My life story is very close to yours Mr. Hicks, and knowing that you made it through a good man, gives me courage.

That's precisely what many struggling teenagers need – a little courage! They probably won't find it at home and it's not likely to come from their circle of friends, but perhaps we could stir it up. Its people just like you and me that can be the bright spot in a young person's life. Take a closer look at the word encourage: "en-*courage*." There it is. It's that simple. It means *"to give someone courage"*.

It's not expensive.

It doesn't hurt to give.

You might be a teacher, a coach, a counselor, a caring adult or a parent. Each of us has the honor of playing doctor, and the prescription is encouragement. Administer morning, noon and night for thirty days, but note the refill order on the bottle. They may need repeated doses. Of course they'll have to trust us, so we'll need to work on building some relational equity. They'll need to believe we understand, so we may have to get a little vulnerable and share some of our story.

Can you see how much power we have to help a struggling teenager, such incredible influence. Why do we hold back? Having an impact, the lasting kind, can be as simple as a timely smile, a well-chosen word or an unexpected action that says, "You matter. You are worthy to be loved. You have value!" It's hard to measure the impact of

> *You have the honor of playing doctor and the prescription is encouragement.*

spoken words of encouragement. We can only imagine what a child feels when we look them in the eye and say, "Do you know what I see when I look at you? I see greatness!"

Like water sprinkled on a parched plant, the roots of apathy drink in these encouraging words and, in short order, the branches above ground begin to perk up. Leaves, once drooping, begin to lift again and reach up toward the sun. They bend toward its warmth and gather its energy. And one day, if we look closely, we will see blossoms, beautiful and full of aroma. Ahhh! When you see blossoms, you know what's coming.

Fruit is on its way.

When that happens, something profound is on the horizon. Beyond the clouds a rainbow is forming.

That's when a storm can become a gift.

Chapter Five

My Storm Is My Gift

****

There's a beautiful thing about storms – they pass. The wind dies down and the sun comes out again. There may be a few branches on the ground and a basket full of leaves in the pool, but storms usually relent. They run their course, do some damage and then fade away into the distance. It's true in nature and it's true in life.

I recall being heartbroken many years ago when a girl I "loved" decided we should just be friends. The emotion of that breakup was pretty overwhelming. I remember my mother calling and how quickly she realized something was wrong. Just hearing her consoling voice on the phone choked me up and I couldn't talk. "Are you Okay?"

"Yep," I answered, in a high-pitched voice.

"Do you want to talk about it?"

"Nope."

"Would you like me to call back later?"

"Yep."

I chuckle about it now, but at the time that was big stuff. I was in a blizzard of hurt and could not have been comforted by Mother Teresa herself. I just needed time. Sure enough, time took care of it. The storm passed and within a few weeks I was "in love" with someone else.

As adults, most of us have figured out that life's mountains are not nearly as tall as they often seem at first. They feel big, no question about it, but they don't look as imposing when you're on the top and looking down. Many a mountain, once scaled, turns out to be the proverbial mole hill.

Please don't get me wrong. I'm not saying the storms that young people face aren't real and painful. Some of the stories they've written about their lives describe horrible events. I shake my head at times and wonder how they've turned out as well as they have, but for many teenagers, the storms that seem so overwhelming will indeed blow over.

Finding companionship, enduring loneliness, resisting peer pressure, surviving family dysfunction – these storms will fade into the horizon one day. They will become part of a distant past. Young storm survivors may end up tattered and even scarred, but as we know, adversity often makes people stronger. The storms of life can lead to greater measures of wisdom and understanding. Even the deep hurt of being abandoned and compromised can leave behind the seeds of extraordinary empathy and compassion for others struggling to endure life's storms.

That's when something truly inspiring can take place – storms can turn into gifts. When the search teams head out to help the victims of life's hurricanes, it is former storm survivors who make the most effective relief workers. If I'm drowning, I want to be rescued by someone who's been in deep water before and knows how to swim.

We need to help struggling young people see their storm can have incredible meaning. They don't have to wear a tattoo on their heart the rest of their lives that says "cursed." Once they get beyond the struggle, they have

> *They don't have to wear a tattoo on their heart the rest of their lives that says "Cursed."*

the potential to become someone else's angel. When storms hit someone else they're often the first ones to plunge back into the rain, the sleet and the snow to rescue those about to go under. It's their hand that extends and beckons to the hurting, "Come on…get up. Don't quit! I've been where you are. You can make it. It may seem dark and impossible right now, but it's not. There is a way through. If you let me, I can help you to the other side."

When people persevere through storms they become uniquely equipped to comfort others. They've been lost in the fog of chaos and know the way through. When they say, "I can help you," they are credible. When they speak words like, "You can make it," they are believable.

As caring adults, we can help the storm-beaten teenager see that their heartache will one day qualify them to be someone's hero.

We might even be able to help them write another chapter in their life history where, on the final page, they declare with resounding confidence,

"My storm is my gift!"

My mother was adopted at birth. She never met her natural mother until she was grown, married and the mother of six of her own children. When they did finally meet, she sat with her birth mother, and for the first time, heard the circumstances behind her adoption. Through tears, her natural mother shared her heartache and what led to the decision to give up her child. She was the product of a rather embarrassing, and not-so-romantic, encounter between her mother and her mother's sister's boyfriend. The boyfriend showed up at a community event and afterwards provided her with a ride home. "He had his way with me," she explained.

Quite a family blowup ensued and nine months later my sweet mother entered the world in the midst of a scandal. She was born in a doctor's office, not a hospital, and her adoption papers were scribbled out on a tablet and signed by the doctor, her natural mother and three witnesses.

To this day, my mother has never met her natural father. It's incredible to me that a child could be given away with so little fanfare. Today, the same process would cost thousands of dollars and a ream of paper for all the documentation.

(Adoption document)

Maysville Arkansas

To whom it may concern,

I Miss Elizabeth [ ], being twenty-one years of age and sound of mind, do hereby for the purpose of adoption, give to Mrs. George McCarty Jr. my daughter Rosanna of my own free will and accord, which was born to me at the home of Dr. Craig in the town of Maysville Ark. I hereby relinquish all claim and right to said child whose name after adoption will be Rosanna McCarty.

Signed, Elizabeth [ ]

I imagine in today's culture, my mother would have been a likely candidate for a terminated pregnancy. And of course, I wouldn't be writing this book if that had happened. That's the point. An awkward and difficult storm left in its wake a beautiful rainbow. There are six of us kids now. Two of my sisters have adopted children of their own, three in all. My mom ended up being raised in a different state, by a different woman. She married her high school sweetheart, my dad, and raised a great family. But parenting didn't stop with her own children. Something compelled her to do more, to extend some love and understanding to a few other confused and troubled teenagers. As a result, more than 90 foster children, nearly all high school age, have called my parents' old farmhouse in Oregon home.

My mom and dad are amazing people, and the ripple effect of their compassion will never be fully known. My mother grew up never having known her natural parents or siblings, but that did not prevent her from having a profound and lasting impact on many others who struggled through similar family storms of their own. My mother is an example of how storm travelers seem to develop a special kind of kinship with each other. Those more fortunate may never fully understand. She is proof that a storm doesn't have to be a never-ending curse. Abandonment, abuse or even rape does not guarantee a life without value. You just never know how things might turn out. The unlikely, and even the seemingly impossible, are often the very conditions from which inspiration and beauty are born. When a struggling teenager opens up to us about their problems we often feel helpless. I mean honestly, what can we really do? We don't usually have the power to change their circumstances outside of school, but we can point to the rainbow on the horizon. We can direct their attention to others who have survived similar storms and share some of those amazing stories. We can help them persevere and see possibilities beyond the dark cloud of the moment.

We can give them hope.

Some days, the most productive thing we might accomplish might have nothing to do with our curriculum. Those are the days we get to help a struggling teen lift his or her head and see some hope beyond the struggle. How many times have we missed that opportunity? How many days were we too preoccupied with our lesson plan, when a timely word of encouragement could have made a profound difference?

You and I have in our hands a powerful gift to offer to the storm travelers who enter our rooms each day. We can help them embrace the idea that they have a gift worth offering too, a gift that could change the world for another struggling soul. It's a gift that is difficult to see when life is hard. It's found in an unlikely place, a place they might never look.

It's found inside their storm.

Chapter Six

Forgiveness

****

I don't think it occurs to teenagers that adults might be storm travelers too. They don't see that we grownups are nothing more than seasoned teenagers with varying degrees of wrinkles. The relentless tug of gravity over the years may have pulled our chest muscles into our mid-sections, but in truth, we're really not that different. Kids don't realize that, like them, adults struggle too! Most of us walk with a limp. Our knees are colored with the purple hue of bruises accrued from our own stumbling over the years. Take a closer look, and you'll see that most of us have abrasions on our hearts as well. The truth is, we all get knocked around along the way in life and the journey leaves many scars, but we survived. Wouldn't it be nice to say that we navigated all of life's storms with grace and humility; that we behaved with courage and flawless integrity? We could say it, but who would believe us? Most of us would have to confess that we didn't face many of our storms admirably. Some of them kicked our butts and left us frazzled and confused. People deal with pain in different ways, but it seems to me that the coping mechanisms tend to follow a similar pattern. Some people medicate with drugs (both prescribed and otherwise) to numb things up for a while and to help them endure. Some take the athletic approach, "ice and elevate." That's code for "chill," literally…and figuratively. Just withdraw and become immobile, and time will heal the wounds. That works well for injured knees and ankles, but not always for broken hearts.

Still others employ the ever-popular treatment known as distraction – my personal favorite. We fill our minds with all manner of things to keep us from thinking about the ache inside. We watch movies, play videogames and plunge into sports, hobbies and noble causes. It all seems quite normal, and yes, it does tend to work … for a while.

> *We don't get mulligans in life; there are no do-overs.*

Others seek distraction in the temporary pleasures of physical indulgences; like sex, eating, exercising, or shopping. People in chaos, hounded by stress and burdened with depression, succumb to a variety of things that can become unhealthy. Unfortunately, there is often collateral damage. Other people get hurt when we don't handle our storms well. Storm travelers can be very selfish people.

Without thinking, we all have a tendency to revise Spock's immortal line in *Star Trek* from: "The needs of the many outweigh the needs of the one," to "The needs of the one [me] outweigh the needs of the many."

When adults don't handle storms well, others around them get damaged too. Let's face it; coping with challenging circumstances is an acquired skill. We're supposed to get better at it with experience. No one picks up a set of golf clubs and shoots par the first time out. There's that pesky water hazard on hole number three and the sand trap on six. And why won't they mow that tall grass on the fringe? I found eight balls over there, and none of them were mine. People *learn* to play golf, but even after years of experience, most folks still play poorly. Dealing with life's storms is no different.

So how about we just accept the truth? We have all screwed up. We have all hurt people, especially those we love the most. While we were drowning, those closest to us were most in danger of being struck by our flailing arms. In our struggle to survive we almost pulled them under with us. Some of those victims may still keep their distance when we come around. They have memories of us, and they're not happy ones. An internal warning light comes on inside them when they see us coming: *"Caution! Potentially Dangerous!"*

All of us recall people we hurt when we were struggling to face one kind of storm or another.

What do we do now?

How do we fix it?

For starters we can do something simple, yet profoundly powerful; we can ask for forgiveness. We don't get mulligans in life; there is no do-overs, but we can acknowledge how badly we behaved. We can humble ourselves and say, "I'm sorry." There might be other things we can do as well to make it right, but it all starts with, "Please forgive me. I was wrong. I was struggling and I handled the storm poorly. I was selfish and I hurt you." This is hard stuff for everyone, including adults. We don't know half the people we've hurt as we have floundered through life. Those we do know about we can try to talk to. The others, we will just have to leave in God's hands.

Asking for forgiveness is a big first step, but it is important to remember that we can't control the responses of others. We can only leave the offering there and mean it with all our hearts. The one we hurt will have to decide what they will do with it. I do know this: There is no gift I have ever received that compares to being forgiven. It's the best news I ever got. When someone you've hurt, even years in the past, says, "I forgive you," it lifts a burden from our shoulders like nothing else can do. It sets us free from a weight of guilt and restores what was broken. It's amazing how quickly relationships can be mended through such simple words.

You might be wondering, "What does this have to do with teachers working with struggling students? Well, here's the thing: teenagers need to learn how to forgive the people who have hurt them. The anger and resentment some of them carry around becomes a tinted window through which they view everything in their lives. Sometimes the bitterness seeps through their pores and is almost visible. You can almost hear the unspoken anger: "I've been screwed and I'm really pissed off about it!" When students in my General Studies classes write their life stories, they often express deep resentment toward the people who have let them down. Without learning how to forgive, that resentment may eat away at them for years to come, and prevent them from moving forward. Here's one example:

My dad showed up out of nowhere. I was shocked but something inside me was very happy. He explained to me why he wasn't there and I accepted it. Hey, I was just happy to see him. I was spending a lot of time with him and not with the thugs I usually hung around with. He was talking to me about stuff and about his other son who looks just like me. The next day it was Thanksgiving. It was night and I saw my uncle and my dad arguing outside the garage so I went over and said, "Yo, Daddy, wassup?" And my dad said, "I have to go back. It was good seeing you. "I felt like my childhood died right then that day. So I called him Luis after that (I didn't call him dad.) After my dad left again, my uncle was talking to me and I just told him, "Hey! It's not like I'm 5 years old. I won't be asking my mom 'When is daddy coming home?' Who needs him? I learned how to fight and play sports without him. I didn't need him then and I don't need him now, but I'm sure as hell not going to abandon my kid like he did." Then I just started crying and said, "How come he doesn't want me?"

Teens look at the adults in their lives and sometimes see some pretty bad behavior. They feel the emptiness of being abandoned and know the hurt of not being loved. Over time, the emotions simmer into bitterness and resentment, eventually coming

64

to a boil and spewing out as anger. We can't make it all okay for them, but we can remind them of an important truth. The adults who let them down are most likely storm travelers too. Some of them were abandoned, hurt and unloved as well. They have their own scars, their own emptiness and their own pain. Kids can be devastated by divorce, for example, but so can the parents. Kids struggle to say no to unhealthy friends, the ones they so desperately need, but adults get lonely too. Kids fall prey to temptation and make horrible, destructive choices, but so do the wrinkled teenagers they call mom and dad.

Take, for example, a teenager struggling with bitterness because of the shortcomings of a parent. When asked to make a list of all the things he or she <u>never</u> received from that parent, what do they record?

No praise or affirmation?

No support and encouragement?

No kindness or tenderness?

No understanding or empathy?

No security or reassurance?

No love?

The truth is, many parents never received those things either when they were growing up. They have their own "Things-I-didn't-get" list.

Adults who had poor role models tend to become poor role models themselves, and dysfunction often passes from generation to generation. Somewhere along the line, the cycle has to stop. Some teens are so angry and bitter with the adults in their lives it's almost palpable and those emotions can be both blinding, and paralyzing. Every interaction with those adults is viewed through the tinted lens of resentment. The hurt festers over time and a mountain of hostility stands before them, an obstacle blocking their progress.

"My storm is my dad. My solution is to shut him out of my life after I graduate from high school. Ever since he came back from Iraq, he's suffered from post-traumatic stress. He has anger problems, constantly threatens me and threatens to kill my puppy almost every day. The only time he's ever happy is when he's miserable. Every one that is close to my dad knows exactly how he is. My mom can't stand him, my brother can't stand him, and neither can I.

What did this father experience during his tour in Iraq? Did he have to take lives? Did he head out in the morning to do his duty only to return at the end of the day and see an empty bunk where a friend and comrade used to sleep? His young son will probably never understand the scars of war. It doesn't excuse his father's bad behavior, but perhaps it would help his son if we could assist him in learning a little about post-traumatic stress disorder and the struggle many vets experience when they come home after a difficult tour? Maybe this son could find a little more grace and extend a little more patience. Maybe we could help him start some conversations with his dad and one day find a way to forgive him.

Another young man wrote:

"OK, I'm a Libra, and a twin. I was born a blond and my twin a redhead. My mom is a scorpion redhead, (scorpions are vengeful people), and she always favored her precious redheaded children. Even my sister noticed. I always thought, and still do, that to get my mom's attention you had to be a redhead. I hate this woman so much. She wonders why my dad has my loyalty and she doesn't. What gumption she has to DEMAND my loyalty when she has shown none to ME!

If this young man holds on to those bitter feelings they will likely hinder his progress, both academically, and in his personal life. Trying to move forward in life while carrying negative emotions like those can be like swimming upstream with a 10-pound weight tied to our ankle.

Learning to forgive can help cut that burden loose!

Struggling young people are quick to point out the flaws in others, but very slow to see their own shortcomings. Sound familiar? As teachers, counselors and caring adults, we can help welcome teenagers to the human race. We can challenge them to be mature beyond their years and encourage them to give grace and forgiveness to those responsible for their storms.

One of my students wrote in his family and school history assignment, about his anger toward his mother. When I met him in my sophomore intervention class he was coming off a horrible freshman year with a 1.08 GPA. He was a smart kid but the roller coaster home life, and the anger bubbling inside him, took center stage and school got pushed to the fringe. My job was to draw him back and get him working at school again. As he wrote his story, pieces of the confusion and chaos in his life poured out on paper.

My story would start off with elementary school. It's nice being the class clown and knowing everyone in school. It's nice being friends with teachers and students, but it sucks when it all gets screwed up.

In second grade I was smart and talked to everyone. I remember my teacher; she was a good combination of chubby and nice. I played tag with 8-10 friends at a time nearly every day and was the second fastest kid in my class. There was only one kid faster than me. I saw him again when I was in the eighth grade. He had become a drug addict who stole bikes from houses and sold them on Craigslist for drug money.

In third grade I stopped talking to friends as often and began not caring for teachers at all. My grades were still average and my friends changed from the popular kids to a hybrid of nerd and cool. This all began when my mother started arguing with my dad. After my mom left, my dad told me, "I could see the crazy in her eyes when she would scream for hours."

In the fourth grade I completely stopped caring about everything. That was the year everything started going to shit. I actually cared so little about school that all my teachers lost hope; this went on through eighth grade and into my freshman year.

In the fifth grade my hair was long and severe anger problems took their course. I can recall sitting in my living room and clenching my throat so tight while growling through glued teeth

68

from random anger. This was when my mom began cheating on my dad. Several different affairs led to their eventual divorce, the last with a seventeen year old boy; my mom was forty-three.

In the sixth grade I remember voluntarily sitting outside my classroom during recess because I hated people. I remember my sister not wanting to get up for school. She would be screaming, kicking and fighting and it would make my anger worse. I remember my dad got hit by my mom during this time and so a fight broke out. I sat by and watched them fight with my brother on my dad's back, hanging off the floor and my sister punching my father's rib cage. Everyone was in the living room screaming. I thought, "If I get their attention they'll stop" so I screamed high pitch and loud, and they did stop, for about 3 seconds, and then they were back at it. I just went to my room and waited for it to end.

Everything got flipped around. Things went from a loving mother and father, to cheating; from a loving brother and wonderful sisters, to the exact opposite. I was young, so I thought "mommy" was the good one, so one day I gave her my baseball bat and she said "thanks." A few minutes later my dad had the bat and was yelling.

My home was full of violence. I even remember one of my sisters, the messed up one, fighting with my mom and punching her in the right eye. It left a ¼ inch cut and my mom left and didn't come back for a day.

During 7ᵗʰ grade I spent my time sitting on a bench under a tree at recess. I wouldn't talk to anyone or do anything; this lasted the whole seventh grade year. I was always the first one to the bench and one day I was sitting there minding my own business when this kid bigger than me walked up and said, "Hey." I said, "Hello" and then he slapped me across the face for no reason, and then left. I had seen so much violence by this time I didn't even care or feel it; I just kept on sitting.

Though I used to be really outgoing when I was younger, I found myself not knowing how to talk to people and, having a popular brother sucked because girls would always walk up to me and talk to me, but I could barely talk back. It made me feel hopeless.

Even though I never did homework the work I did occasionally complete got A's or B's. I knew I was smart, but I was just completely lost and angry at everything. My first fight happened when a kid tripped me while I was running off the bus chasing one of my very few friends. I got up and stared at his face, and then, without thinking, I punched his left eye. He then tackled me and pinned me to a seat. I just wanted to rip his throat out so I grabbed his Adam's apple and dug in and began to pull. He jumped off and that ended the fight, but my anger boiled with such intensity that when I got home I grabbed my bat and started hitting my dad's practice boxing dummy over and over again. I was in a blind fury when my dad came out and tried to stop me, but I didn't want to calm down. Instead, loving the adrenaline, I ran to the back yard. When I did finally calm down I sat on the roof of my house for an hour and then went inside and slept.

In the eighth grade my anger subsided slightly and my grades went from all F's to F's and a few D's. I also gained a group of friends to hang out with, but none of them were pot heads or alcoholics; they were good kids. Being surrounded by weed and alcohol every day by my brother, and constantly rejecting it, gets hard after a while so I finally gave in and smoked for the first time in my backyard with my brother and two of his friends. I liked weed, but did not smoke again for three months. After my second time with my brother I started liking it because it helped me with my anti-socialness. I started "fitting in" and by the end of my eighth grade year I was smoking and drinking twice a week.

To this day though, I still hate my brother. He beat me up on my ninth birthday. I didn't have too many friends, so he asked if he could invite some of his friends to my party and I said yes. I got two new video games that day but my brother and his friends played them for a long time. Eventually I started whining and asking if I could play. Finally, I turned off the X-box. Immediately my brother got up and punched me in the face. I fell on a travel bag and the metal bar was crushing my left cheek because his knee was digging into my neck. After the fight was done I went into my parent's room and lay next to their bed on the floor and cried. Finally, after three hours, his friends left.

> **The day is fast approaching when I will lose my mind.**

About this time things got crazy with my parents. My dad found out that my mom was regularly taking thousands of dollars *out of their savings account and using it to buy houses in her home country. She bought three houses in all, and 25 acres of land. She also bought over $8000 worth of sex toys and tried selling them for a profit. When that failed she left them in the closet of their bedroom. During this time she spent money on a surgery on her breasts and between her legs and there were many other purchases I don't know about. All I know is my father is literally paying for it all now and my brother and my dad and I are living pay-check to pay-check just to survive. As if things couldn't be worse, I get to hear my father tell me nearly every day how much of a whore my mom is; how she is an "evil, slutty, stupid insane bitch" and how much he hates her. It used to bother me, but not now, because I know it's true, and I know that I will never love her. As I look back at my life I see a lot of outbursts of anger that have gotten people hurt.*

When I was six, I threw a toy at my brother and gave him a black eye. When I was eight I threw a toothpaste tube at my sister and hit her in the face, forcing her skin into her braces. It took my parents five minutes to get her skin free, tearing it in the process. When I was eleven I threw a sharp pencil at my brother and popped a whole straight through his bottom lip. My brother and I fought constantly, but recently I stopped fighting back. I suppose that isn't healthy either because then all my anger builds up. He just tells me to shut up or I'll get my ass beat. One time, my brother was cleaning out the garage and accidently threw out some new sand paper. When my dad got home he saw it and got mad, so my brother started mouthing off. A minute later I look through the window of my bedroom and see my dad on top of my brother and his arm coming up to hit him. Immediately, I ran to my room and got my bat. Then I ran outside and cracked my dad in the back with it. That made him stop hitting my brother and he left for a while.

The day is fast approaching when I will lose my mind.

*My freshman year was a little better. I still have a burning hatred for school and most people. I'm now a sophomore and this class is the only smart thing that any school has ever done. If I was ever to be a teacher I would fight tooth and nail to force whoever is in charge to create this class at every school in the United States of f***ed-up, shit ass America.*

It didn't take long before I bumped into this young man's volatile anger. I noticed right away that it lurked just beneath the surface and the simple act of prodding him to open his binder and get started on an assignment, could trigger an outburst. Some of the outbursts couldn't be tolerated, and I had no choice but to write a few referrals to the Dean's office. Gradually however, we began to have some conversations about his anger and how it was getting in the way of his success in school. Little by little, I built some trust, and relational equity began to accrue.

One day we had a breakthrough. After a mild explosion, and some time to calm down, I called him to the chair I keep near my desk. I asked him to tell me a little about his mom and her upbringing. He explained that she was raised in a family with 13 children in a large city in Central America. Life was hard for her family. They were poor, and with a lot of time spent on the streets, she didn't get to go to school very much. We talked about her life in America and her promiscuous behavior. And then I asked him a question he didn't expect to hear. "If your mom had been in a class like this when she was sixteen, what do you think she would have written in her life story assignment? Have you ever wondered what her life was like when she was your age? Being on the streets, poor and uneducated, have you thought about what she did to survive? Did she have to sell her body? Could she have been abused and taken advantage of? Did her hard life somehow warp her ideas about what was normal and good with men?"

He listened and I could see the wheels turning in his head.

Perhaps for the first time he began to consider that maybe his mom had storms of her own. Maybe he was right, she was screwed up, but there were reasons…there were roots to her dysfunction as a wife and mom, just like there were roots to his anger and apathy as a student. From that day forward I began to see a change. His issues became less about hating his mom, and more about controlling his anger when it came to the surface. Academically, a light came back on and he began caring about school again. As the anger gradually dissipated, his characteristic scowl was replaced by a happier countenance and frequent smiles. What used to trigger an outburst of anger became easily managed with a little humor. "Hey, don't blow up on me dude or I'll flog you with my yarn ball." Instead of hearing mumbled expletives, I'd see a grin, and then a binder opened and pencil moving.

At the end of the school year I asked this young man to write again.

I would say a lot has changed since the beginning of the year. I believe I changed partly because I matured more, but that's just part of it. The second reason is I got over my anger, and when I did, the depression faded away also. I never really started making quick progress until someone helped me realize why I was angry. When you realize that everyone has suffered, and that their suffering changes them, you realize that maybe those changes have caused them to make a lot of bad decisions. Once you make a conscious decision to forgive, and literally forget, you are able to be happy, but it's not always a quick process.

Someone once said that failing to forgive is like drinking a cup of poison every day and expecting the other person to die. The truth is, that by refusing to forgive others, we destroy ourselves. Forgiving is not always predicated by an apology. What if they never ask? Will it help the situation to keep marinating in bitterness until they do?

Some of the struggling young people we work with are shackled in a prison of bitterness, resentment and anger, and they will never get free unless they learn how to forgive. Helping them learn that important truth could be the most important lesson we teach all year. Why? Because on the journey toward healing, forgiveness is often where the trail begins.

Chapter Seven

Divorce: My Family is Broken

✸✸✸✸✸✸✸✸✸✸✸✸✸✸✸✸✸✸✸✸

There is something deeply important about having our two birth parents together and in the home with us. Mom and Dad are supposed to be united, to be "one." It took them both, in a moment of intimacy, to make us. They chose in that moment to exercise a sacred power—to create a human being. We are the result of that miraculous moment. We grew and stirred inside the safety of our mother's womb until the day we entered this strange new world. There, staring down at us, were two pairs of gleaming eyes with smiles spread across two happy faces that seem to say:

"Hello son. Hello daughter. We're your parents. Welcome to the family."

What a profound moment! Being born into a family gives us a place where we knew we belong. Not only are we safe in our helplessness, we have roots, heritage and history. From our very birth we are a part of a distinct line, a branch on a well-established tree, and as a result, we are secure, surrounded by a kind of safety and wholeness that provides the best of worlds for a child to grow up in. There is nothing as natural as two parents, together, happily in love with each other, and bringing children into the world. That's the way it's supposed to be, isn't it? That's normal, right?

Reality check!

We know that's not always the case. In fact, more than half of today's marriages don't survive, and before they fail, there are often little souls in the mix. The sad truth is, broken vows often create broken children. What makes divorce even more heartbreaking and difficult for a child is the finality of the situation. Once a family unit is severed, and the adults move on to other relationships, the brokenness can never be fully mended.

Coming home every day to a family that is intact and secure is a great comfort to a child. They belong somewhere and to someone, but for many of the struggling students we teach, that secure structure does not exist. For them, living in a "broken home" has become the norm and wounds can remain that are difficult to heal. A silent yearning often lingers for what might have been—for what should have been. At some point the questions come:

"Why was I robbed of my family?"

"Why couldn't they keep us together?"

"Why do I have to choose between mom and dad?"

"Why couldn't I have a normal home?"

"Who do I belong to, anyway?"

"Why did he leave?"

"How could she forget me?"

"Was it my fault?"

"Is there something wrong with me?"

"If my own parents could abandon me, how can I ever trust anyone else not to leave?"

These kinds of questions, and a thousand more, can shake the very foundation of a child's world. From the security of a strong family unit most children will flourish, but more times than not, a broken family fractures the child. With no voice in the matter they find themselves in a refugee camp along with other storm survivors, hunkered down, hurt, and trying to endure the confusion. This is not the life they envisioned for themselves and despite other positive influences around them, they often feel strangely incomplete. Divorce can

> ***More times than not, a broken family breaks the child.***

be like a death in the family where the grieving never quite ends. But unlike a death, there can be no real closure. The constant bouncing back and forth between custodians often keeps the wounds raw and painful. The hurt of this unfixable situation can turn into anger and manifest as rebellion. The heart shouts back at the parents, "Why should I care about what you want? You didn't care about my needs. Your divorce ruined my life and destroyed my security and now you want me to care about your feelings? Welcome to the hurt! How does it feel?" Students dealing with a broken home, or its aftermath, display a complicated combination of problems. It may take years for them to sort through their feelings and recover from the storm.

As caring adults we may get distracted by the outward symptoms we see, but when we follow the threads back to their origin we often arrive at a familiar place—a disrupted family unit. School and life were going along just fine for the child and then devastation hit. Mom and dad got caught in a storm of their own, and they couldn't get through it. Perhaps ill-equipped themselves, they couldn't persevere and the storm pulled them apart. Being tugged in two directions, children can lose touch with who they are and where they belong in the world. They become collateral damage. Like the baby bird in P.D. Eastman's book, "Are You My Mother?" who, after falling from its nest, wandered about aimlessly asking the question, "Are you my mother?" Neither the cat, the hen, the dog, the cow, the car, the boat, the plane, nor even the excavator could say "yes". Finally, the bird cries out, "Where am I? I want to go home. I want my mother!"

For the baby bird, the story ends happily. The baby ends up back in the nest, its mother returns with its dinner and all is well. Not so with children enduring a divorce. When the nest falls apart, there is disorientation. Life will never be the same. There is no going "home."

Teenagers have a unique way of expressing their feelings. Their words are often simple, yet revealing. What follows are a few of their stories. As you read, watch for the survival techniques they employ. Listen to their hearts and imagine how they have felt. Crawl into their shoes just a little and you will understand why school has lost its appeal and why the dark cloud of apathy has settled over their souls.

In these stories, I have highlighted some key phrases and assigned numbers to them. The numbers correspond to the chart at the end of the chapter that identifies some of the recurring roots of apathy. Keep in mind, there are many other circumstances, in addition to divorce, that can result in a broken family. Sometimes it's incarceration, military service, even a death in the family. The result is often some kind of blended family situation that creates challenges for kids. Young people respond to family brokenness in a variety of ways and when we try to unravel the mess one thing quickly becomes apparent: it's complicated!

*"In the first and second grade I was known as the smartest kid in the class. I was already reading at a high level and doing some simple algebra. I got straight A's in 3rd grade, but ¹**then** toward the end of the year my parents were heading for a divorce and ²**it really hit me hard**. I understood why they decided to separate, but it still messed me up. I can remember in 3rd grade having to jump on my dad to try and keep him from hitting my mom, so I guess it was for the best.*

*My 4th grade year was the year my parents divorced. This was ²**one of the hardest years** because my parents were in a ³**custody battle** for me and my little brother and we always had them telling us how bad the other parent was. ⁴**But I fell in love with football** and ever since that's all I've cared about...besides taking* care of my little brother. We lived at my mom's house most of the time and we visited my dad because of his work schedule, but my mom worked a lot too, Mondays through Saturdays from 7am–6pm. So me and my brother were *5alone a lot* of the time.

My 6*th* grade year *2got pretty difficult*. My mom was constantly bringing *8new guys* in and out of the house, but *5never really had time for us kids.* Junior high was by far my *2worst year* in my school history. I started selling and doing *4drugs* that year. My *6GPA was at 0.9* and I was constantly in the office for *7behavior issues.* This was my first year being *6taken out of football* because of my grades. It was when I was taken out of football that I got *4heavily involved in the drug life*. With my mom always involved with *8other guys* and my dad trying to make *8his [new] marriage* work *5I felt unwanted*. That was one of the main reasons *9I started my brotherhood*. It felt like family and we knew we'd always have each other's backs.

During my 8*th* grade year my *3mom lost custody* of me and my little brother and we *10moved* in with our dad and his *8new wife*. We *11fight a lot* so from then until now I've been *10back and forth* between my dad and my grandma. They had me in a private school for a while, but now I'm here.

5I feel alone: *10new school, new house* and *5no friends*. It's like *5I have no one to watch my back or talk to*. It's me against the world. The weird thing is, I kind of like it that way. When you *12trust* people, you can be let down. And I hate being let down time after time."

No wonder kids from broken homes are so hard to figure out and help. Where do we start? They may have abandonment issues, anger issues and behavior issues, both at home (however "home" is defined) and at school. To numb the hurt they seek belonging and distraction in various ways that can leave them dealing with regret, shame, unworthiness and failure. Permeating it all is a loss of trust in people, especially adults who profess to care about them.

Some of you may be familiar with this young man's loneliness. You know about that anxious feeling of uncertainty that looms like a cloud over all your hopes and aspirations.

What will become of me?

Who has my back now?

Will I have a safety net if life gets hard?

Where is home?

If you have a story like this young man, take a minute, and find those memories again. Go back in time and let those emotions stir within you and rise to the surface. As you relive those feelings, think of the young people sitting in your classroom who are in the storm of family brokenness right now. You made it through those difficult experiences; you weathered the storm and survived, but for their sakes, don't forget what it was like. Your empathy and understanding may uniquely qualify you to be the very one that can pull them through. Dare to share that piece of your story. Just knowing that you, a caring, successful, loving adult, survived the heartache of a broken home, can bring hope to a despairing young person. If you made it through and turned out so well, perhaps they can make it too.

Another student wrote:

"When I got to middle school everything changed. All of a sudden my dad planned to move us all to Texas. So, halfway through the school year, we packed up our clothes and furniture, and moved. After we got everything settled, I started going to middle school. Everyone befriended me and referred to me as the "new girl." I made a lot of new friends, and to be honest, I didn't think that would happen. Going into my 7th grade year I got involved at school and joined the dance team. It was an indoor campus with really cool teachers and I liked this school more than anything. [1]Then one day my sister and I were minding our own business; just sitting in her room, when out of nowhere my dad rushed in the room and started bawling hysterically. He told us that my mom wanted to file for divorce. After a week went by, we [10]moved back to California and I started attending a new junior high. [10]I lived with my dad, brother, aunt, uncle and three of their kids. None of us had any communication at all with my mom. When I started realizing that they were really getting a divorce I was in the 8th grade.

"That was the year I started [7]getting in trouble. I [11]rebelled against my dad, started [7]getting suspended and hung out with the [13]wrong people. I [14]didn't care about anything at all. The summer before starting high school it got bad. [13]I got into things that weren't the right thing to do. Freshman year I started communicating with my mom and started [11]arguing with her. Once again, I [14]didn't care

83

about anything. I got [7]suspended three times and I [6]didn't do anything in my classes. Sophomore year I [6/14]didn't care what grades I got, what my teachers did, or anything. I started [6]failing all my classes. I also started [15]not coming to school. It was so bad to the point that I only went to 7th period once a month or so. [14] I hated coming to school because my personal problems at home conflicted with school so much.

In this story we see many of the telltale signs of struggle. School was a happy place until the family breakup; then came the move, and the disrupted life. Trouble at school soon followed, and then rebellion at home. It didn't take long for "wrong friends" to enter the picture and with them some poor choices.

Among other things, the prevailing attitude is captured well in the phrase, "I didn't care." Discouraged and helpless to change the situation, this student began to give up. In her own words, she stopped caring about anything—apathy. That's when school attendance and academic progress fell off the cliff and into the abyss.

One more:

"When I was in elementary school, my mom met my step-dad. I loved him so much. They were together 5 years, then they got married. It was the end of my fourth grade year. My step-dad was my life, my best friend. He was more of a dad than my real dad. I started fifth grade year and I loved my teacher. [1]Then halfway through my fifth grade year my mom and my step-dad divorced. I was really [2]upset. My [5]best friend had left and I felt really alone.

The only thing I really remember was walking in the door and seeing my step-dad's swords gone and I thought that we had got the house we bid on. My mom told me that my step-dad had left. I remember every night for a long time calling him and [5]begging him to come home. Camp Keep [school environmental camp] came around and I hadn't stayed the night anywhere since everything happened. [2]I cried a lot being there. [12]I had really bad trust issues. Summer came and went and it was time to start 6th grade. The day I started school I didn't want my mom to leave me there [5/12]because I was afraid she wouldn't come back."

This story adds another interesting twist. It's the departure of a step-parent that creates the trauma. The new man in her mom's life turned out to be a great guy. He was more sensitive and caring than the birth father. He filled the void and brought back a measure of wholeness. The family unit was restored. But then it happened again. He leaves!

Disappointment and heartbreak return. At first she tries to fix it. She begs him to come back, but it's over, and that old feeling of aloneness and abandonment camp out on her doorstep once again. It comes as no surprise when she writes, *"I had really bad trust issues."* Even mom's love is now questioned. *"Could she leave me, too? Will she be there when I get home from school?"*

The breakup of a family leads to an array of emotions underpinned by fear, confusion, and uncertainty. After the initial shock of the breakup, it's all about coping, and survival mode kicks in. Kids can't control the situation, so enduring it becomes the only course of action. It may take years to overcome the feelings of abandonment and kids in these circumstances frequently struggle with trusting others. Life has taught them a harsh lesson: getting attached to people can be very painful.

As educators, we cannot put the pieces of a broken home back together again, but we can listen to their stories and validate their struggle. We can show them that we understand and care and that can be huge. Just acknowledging how normal it is to be apathetic about school during traumatic times at home can be a source of great encouragement and comfort. It helps the struggling student immensely to know, that under the circumstances, they are actually quite normal.

Some of you reading these pages were also touched by a divorce growing up. You may even have a few scars remaining to show for it. Share some pieces of your story with your students. It can establish a huge connection with a struggling teen and cause your stock on the credibility scale to skyrocket. Your openness about your own struggle could pay big dividends in your relational equity accounts. Why? Because you struggled in the past like they are now, and you turned out okay.

<u>Responses to Divorce</u>

1. Then   the divorce event

2. Impact   the storm begins / emotional trauma

3. Custody   turmoil of two homes

4. Distraction   filling the emptiness / numbing the pain.

5. Loneliness   abandoned / alone

6. Academic Downturn   GPA drop / ineligibility

7. Acting Out   behavior problems / school discipline

8. Other Adults   boyfriends / step parents

9. Belonging   finding another "family" or support group

10. Moved   uprooted / displaced / "homelessness"

11. Rebellion   conflict / fight a lot / argue

12. Trust Issues   fear of being hurt again

13. Unhealthy Friends   desire for companionship

14. Loss of Motivation   apathy / depression

15. Attendance Issues   truancy / absenteeism / tardiness

Chapter Eight

The Party Train

****

It was my sophomore year when I sowed my wild oats and dabbled in a few of the mind-altering substances popular in my day. I really can't point to one thing in particular that led to that season of wandering; it was a combination of things. I suspect that's the case for most teens today who find themselves drawn into the party life. I did have some "storms" at home; I could blame that, but I was also a curious kid. Maybe that should be the prime suspect. Above all else was the very strong and very normal desire to have friends. When my best friends beckoned me to follow them down that unfamiliar and forbidden path, it was nearly impossible to resist. I can vividly recall my buddy prodding me for weeks to go with him and try smoking pot. I had always been on the inside of my small circle of friends, but as they drifted off into this new adventure of getting high it felt like the train was leaving the station and I had been left behind. Joining them, however, meant I had to abandon some deep values that had been ingrained in me from childhood. I had been warned. I knew about the evils and dangers of alcohol and drug use, but now my friends were telling me a different story. They assured me, "The hot burner doesn't hurt when you touch it. Check it out…it's warm. You won't get fried. Look! We've been doing it and we're fine. Our parents are clueless; they don't know what they're talking about. This is fun dude, you gotta try it."

It wasn't really the pressure to join the crowd that hounded me the most, but the fear of being left out. My friends were all enjoying time together with their new best friend. His name was Weed. Everyone kind of knows that he's a bad guy, and to be honest, not too many teens hang out with him all by themselves, at

> *We came together every day at school for our "life sucks" support group and consoled each other.*

least not at first. But when there's a whole group "chilling" with Weed, he doesn't seem so bad. He makes you laugh a lot and helps you forget the crap in your life. Weed was a friend you smoked, and just holding him between your thumb and forefinger was really cool. But he had other companions too, things you drank that made you giddy. They were forbidden also, but none-the-less fun. It all tasted horrible, but that wasn't the point. It was the buzz, and of course, the coolness of it all. Passing a joint around and sharing some brewskies with your friends—it doesn't get any better than that, right?

There's no doubt our parents would never have approved of such activities, but let's be honest. Their approval was not paramount for those of us at the tender age of 15. They were idiots, of course. Besides, there's a kind of fraternity among the rebellious that unites them as they dabble together in the "forbidden." My friends understood me. We came together every day at school for our "life sucks" support group and consoled each other. Of course, in our eyes, we were all dreadfully abused children. We had to do chores, haul hay in the summer, change irrigation pipes, feed cows, build fences, and even clean our rooms! Sometimes we were forced to cut firewood, and some of us even had mandatory homework and passing grades requirements. What were our parents thinking? In our eyes it was like Nazi Germany all over again and life on the farm was nothing more than a concentration camp.

Eventually, the other abused teenagers in my little peer group started adding mind-altering substances to the therapy and I was very tempted to enter the treatment program. I resisted for quite a while, but eventually I gave in.

I joined the crowd.

"Dude, when you kept telling us no, you made us feel about this big," my buddy said, holding his thumb and index finger about an inch apart, *"but now it's cool."*

Wow! Imagine that. My refusal to include myself in their bad decisions made my friends feel uncomfortable. They were actually relieved when I violated my conscience, compromised my values and participated with them. They say misery loves company. For us, it wasn't misery really, but rebellion.

One thing is sure. Once I joined in, it wasn't easy to get out. It was not physical addiction that held me like it is for some, but the prospect of losing my friends…of being alone. I'm convinced the need for companionship is one of the primary reasons many teens are sucked into the party culture. Friends are everything, and being alone can be the worst of all curses. Without support at home and a strong family unit, there is almost no compromise a struggling teen won't make if it provides belonging. One student put it this way:

"It's too late to pick new friends. Kids are mean. Kids are not accepting. No one else can replace my friends. And I cannot, will not, be alone."

Another said:

"Friends are all I basically have. Without them, I really don't know what I would do. Friends are honestly everything."

In the many stories I've read where students describe how they got involved in using drugs and alcohol, it nearly always begins within the context of friendship. The need to belong is such a strong force during adolescence that the choice of who to hang out with becomes critical. Even good kids from good homes feel the pinch and pressure.

"I've always been a pretty good student but in 6th grade I chose a bad friend who had older siblings who were involved in gangs and drugs. My friend invited me over before school one day so we could walk together. We were sitting in her room and it was getting close to the time for school to start. I was getting worried because I was afraid we were going to be late, but I didn't want to say anything because I didn't want her to think I wasn't cool. Five minutes before we were supposed to be at school her brother walked

in with a few of his friends. He was an 8th grader. The next thing I knew she was asking me if I wanted to smoke weed with them before we went to school. I didn't really know what to say so I just said yeah, partly because I didn't want her to think I wasn't cool enough to hang out with them and also because I was curious. We got to school late, but I didn't really feel very different, like, I couldn't tell if I was high or not. That was my first time."

> **Teens who party become masters of deceit.**

Adults like to think teenagers are naïve, but sometimes I think it's the parents who have their heads in the sand. We like to think that we can trust our little angels. After all, we've raised them to know better, right? Maybe so, but the pull to fit in is often stronger than we realize. Given the right (or wrong) opportunity with those highly esteemed peers staring at them, it's very difficult to say no. If a teen does happen to muster the courage to stand their ground, they will often wear down and weaken over time, especially given repeated opportunities.

Let's read more of this girl's story.

"The next time I made some mistakes was in the 8th grade. I had good friends but I liked to hang out with my older brother and his friends—he always had very attractive friends. Everyone likes to hang out with older kids because they look up to them."

Ah, the lure of older kids, especially those of the opposite sex. It's social suicide to look foolish or uncool in their presence.

One day we were all hanging out down the street from their house. They were all smoking cigarettes, which I thought was so-o-o gross. But then they pulled out a pipe and started smoking weed. They asked me if I wanted to hit it and I said sure. I figured, why not? I already did it before. It's not gonna kill me if I do. After that day I'd be smoking weed like at least once a month."

After that initial compromise it becomes easier and easier to repeat bad choices.

"My freshman year I had very good friends and none of them were the type to party or do bad things. But after school I'd walk home with my brother and his friends and this led to bad decisions. I started smoking weed maybe two times a week. To me I didn't notice a change in myself. I was still getting good grades

> **Somehow I always knew my crooked ways would be found out and it put a strain on me.**

and going to church on Wednesday nights and every Sunday. So I was pretty much thinking I was still a good kid. Halfway through the year, I switched to a new high school and made friends quickly. Unfortunately I made friends with the wrong crowd.

<u>*It seemed to me that the bad kids were much more inviting than the good ones.*</u> *So I started hanging out with these kids, not only at school, but outside of school. They would invite me to go to parties with them, invite me to go smoke with them, invite me to ditch school with them, but none of them ever invited me to go to church with them. That should have been a sign to me right there."*

The draw into the party world is usually a slow process. It begins with small compromises and escalates over time. Eventually a teenager's identity, their very self-image, becomes associated with the culture of drugs and alcohol. Along with it often comes sex, rebellion against authority and, in most cases, a significant drop in academic performance. When there is a school change, they quickly identify with others who like to party. It's comfortable territory, so naturally they gravitate to those familiar circles. It's a hard cycle to break, especially during the adolescent years, when finding a group and fitting in are so important. In later years, when

> *During my rebellious period in high school, I felt like I was two different people inside of one skin.*

maturity has taken root, young adults may see the folly of their partying ways, but, unfortunately, by then opportunities may have come and gone. Some teens never quite recover.

During my rebellious period in high school, I felt like I was two different people inside of one skin. I had my party friends on one hand and I had my family, who didn't have a clue about my dark side, on the other. There was fun to be had with my partying buddies, and our new pal Weed, but there was lying and guilt—and of course, the constant fear of being found out.

This brings up an interesting side effect of drug and alcohol use. Teens who party must, by necessity, become masters of deceit. Lying becomes a way of life to keep the secrets hidden. That was the thing that wore me down my sophomore year. I had always perceived myself to be a good person, but using drugs forced me to lie, constantly. My parents would have 'killed' me if they had found out what I was doing. They would also have been very disappointed. To prevent the exposure of my hidden party life, I became a master at crafting stories and explanations.

I love an old Jewish proverb found in the Bible (Proverbs 10:9). It hits the nail on the head.

Whoever walks in integrity

walks securely,

But he who makes his ways crooked

will be found out.

When I was making bad choices and rebelling against the values that I had been raised with, I lived in a state of subtle, but constant fear. I was always concerned that I would be discovered and anxious about what would happen if I got caught. I was worried at school and worried at home. I always had to be sure my stories made sense and that one lie didn't conflict with another. In other words, I was miserable. Somehow I always knew my crooked ways would be found out and that put immense strain on me. There was a lot hanging in the balance. If I got caught at school, I could get kicked out. This was a small town and my dad was a teacher and coach at the high school. If I got expelled for drugs, it would shame and embarrass my whole family. I would also be ineligible to play sports, and they were huge in my life. I had already won a state title in wrestling as a freshman and, with three years to go, I could have a bright college career ahead of me. All that could be jeopardized if I got busted. It all broke for me one night during my sophomore year. I had just told a bunch of lies to my parents. I went upstairs and dropped on my bed in the dark. Staring at the ceiling, I did something I had not done in a long time—I said a prayer. It was more like a plea.

"God, please help me change."

Navigating the fragile line between the two people I was trying to be was exhausting. The internal tug-of-war had to end. I knew exposure was only a matter of time and I resolved then and there it would be better to "fess up" than be found out. I also missed the person I used to be. That's when I had a strange thought; an inclination so odd that I believed it to be an answer to my prayer. It was crystal clear. If I truly wanted to change, I would need to take an extraordinary step. With that in mind I got up from my bed, went to the top of the stairs, and called down to my parents.

"Mom, Dad. Can you come up to my room? I need to talk to you."

I had never done that before, so I imagine they must have looked across the front room at each other and thought *"What the hell's going on?"* By the time they reached my room I had started to cry, but I felt compelled to tell them the truth. Over the next few minutes, I spilled it all out, the lying, the drugs, the ditching class to get high—everything. By the end of my grand confession my mom was crying too, and my dad, well, he was a bit disgruntled, but that day everything truly did change for the better.

It felt so good to do the right thing again and that good feeling gave me strength. I slept peacefully for the first time in months. The proverb was true; when you walk in integrity (do the right thing) you feel secure (peace of mind). The corner had been turned. For nearly two months following that night my friends pestered me to join them as before, but things were different. I had jumped tracks; I was on a new train, heading in a new direction and I didn't want to go back. They couldn't understand the sudden change in me and I couldn't really explain it either. I wasn't able to articulate, at that point, the reasons for my sudden transformation. I just knew I hadn't felt good about myself in a long time. My new

> *An immeasurable number of dreams has been derailed by the party train.*

passion was to stay in that peaceful place and to earn my parents' trust back. After a few months my friends stopped pestering me, but they didn't stop partying. The train went on without me and I was alone, but I was okay with it. Hindsight has taught me it's much harder to get off the party train than it ever was to get on.

Some months later, my former best friend, with whom I used to ditch school and smoke pot, drove his jeep off a steep embankment with another guy and two girls inside. One of the most popular students in our high school died in that accident. She had been my table partner in typing class the year before and a stat girl/cheerleader for the wrestling team. She was a really close friend and I was heartbroken, along with the entire school and community.

Sobering to me now is the fact that if I had not gotten off the party train when I did, I could have been in that jeep too.

A year later, three other former best friends were in another car that left the road and ran under the trailer of a parked eighteen-wheeler. All were seniors, varsity athletes and popular kids in our graduating class of only forty-five students. Two of them died that day. At one parent's request, I helped carry their son's casket from the hearse to his gravesite. What a tragic day that was. Two lives snuffed out in a needless accident. I could have been in that car as well.

Drugs and alcohol typically leave a trail of devastation behind them. The beer advertisements seem to forget that part. The party culture in junior high and high school can provide a lot of fun, excitement, and belonging, but it can also rob young people of their dreams—sometimes even their very lives. Of course most teenagers who jump on the party train are not mature enough to see it for what it truly is at the time. In later years, most acknowledge how foolish and reckless they once were, but the sad truth is that some of them may not make it that far. Those who do survive often find themselves in a deep, academic hole.

Teachers, coaches and counselors see this pattern all the time: the kid with amazing potential who couldn't stay eligible, or the one who never made it to graduation. Many times the patterns of behavior developed during the teen years have a huge impact on future opportunities. There is no question that an immeasurable number of dreams has been derailed by the ever-popular party train.

I saw this played out in vivid fashion as a high school wrestling coach. Many years before my school coaching gig began, one of my sons gave the sport a try, and to my delight, he liked it. Starting at age six he began attending club practices with me two evenings a week at a nearby gym and competing at Saturday age-group tournaments. Along for the ride came one of his best six-year-old buddies. For nearly twelve years I was their only coach. As they grew up and became more accomplished, we traveled to various state and national events and, by their junior year in high school, both were on the radar in state rankings. My son's friend was actually the better of the two at that point and was expected to place in the upcoming state tournament in Rabo Bank Arena in Bakersfield, California. It's not easy to make it to the state tournament in California because it's one of only a few states in the country that has only one division for wrestling. Every wrestler, in every corner of that huge state, enters the grueling three-week process in mid-February. Only forty qualify for the final tournament in early March. The extravaganza begins on a Friday and culminates in a one-mat spectacle on an elevated stage under a spotlight in front of five thousand screaming spectators.

Although my son was numbered among the top fifteen in his weight division his junior year, his friend was ranked much higher and actually stood a chance to occupy that center stage. For a junior, that would have been an incredible achievement. But the opportunity never came. Three weeks before the state meet, on the night before the league tournament, when most good wrestlers are cutting weight and preparing for the big day, this young man made a bad decision. He chose to party with some friends. The next morning, for the first time in eleven years, he failed to make weight. His season came to an abrupt end that morning and the news spread rapidly through the wrestling community.

I was in shock. This kid was like a son to me and I couldn't get the emptiness in the pit of my stomach to go away. When the league tournament came to an end, I got a call from his family. They invited me to an intervention of sorts at his home. He was in trouble with drugs and his reckless behavior was becoming dangerous. We surrounded him with love and support, but it wasn't enough to turn him in a new direction. The rest of the school year, through the summer, and into the fall of his senior year, he continued to ride the party train. Those of us who loved him tried to draw him away from his reckless path, yet he continued. When the next season rolled around he was not the same, mentally or physically. He never won another tournament or received a ranking. In the end, he didn't even qualify to be among the forty at the California State tournament. It was heartbreaking to watch this young man being robbed by those notorious dream-stealers: drugs and alcohol.

I look back now and can't help but notice the two glaringly different paths my son and his childhood buddy traveled. My son finished his senior year with a 48–0 record and the great honor of competing under that spotlight on that elevated stage in front of five thousand screaming fans. His friend watched from somewhere within the recesses of the dark arena. The following year, my son was attending a university on a wrestling scholarship while his friend lived at home, partying, wrecking cars, and losing one job after another. I lost track of him for several years, but heard that he was deeply into a life-threatening drug addiction. It saddened me greatly and I often wondered where he was and how he was doing.

Then one day, while I was teaching my General Studies class, he walked through the door of my classroom bearing a visitor's pass. I was elated to see him. He walked up to me and we embraced in front of thirty students who had no idea who he was. As they worked on an assignment, he and I sat and visited near my desk. I learned that while my son was finishing up his fourth year of college and preparing to enter into a master's program, his friend had been incarcerated for driving under the influence of heroin. He had been out of jail for only a few months and was in a twelve-step program for his addiction. That day he wanted to come by and let me know he was doing all right.

With his permission, I had him stay and tell his story to my next class. Tears welled up in my eyes as he shared about his poor choices with drugs and alcohol, and how his dreams had been set back for nearly six years while he rode the party train. His aspirations and initiative had been numbed as he traded self-discipline and responsibility for fun and the passing pleasures of temporary gratification. He had been a good student early in high school and easily achieved A's and B's, but the last two years he admitted to skating by, doing the absolute minimum in order to graduate. That's apathy; that 'I don't care' attitude that nearly always accompanies those who travel on the party train. Sadly, his story is all too common in our schools today. Unfortunately kids don't see the glaring truth that partying often leads them into a cloud that settles over their soul and steals their dreams. Without even noticing, they stop caring about a lot of things that really matter. One student captured it well:

"When I got into junior high, I started going everywhere my mom didn't want me to go. I started lying to her about where I was and who I was with all the time, almost every day. I became defiant and a rebel to the law and my parents. I got suspended about 8 or 9 times and got kicked out of school the week before the year was over. When I got into high school, I was confused about everything and felt weird, but I had a lot of friends. I started smoking weed and doing some things that got me into a lot of trouble. It took me away from caring about school. At first I hated school a little, but eventually I hated it a lot. I acted crazy sometimes. I disrespected my family and lied constantly."

A significant number of teenagers we work with will dabble in the party life during their high school years. Though they don't let on however, I believe many of them do respect some of the teachers, counselors and coaches in their life, and will listen when we speak some truth to them. They won't always change and jump from the party train all at once, but our message remains with them. And sometimes, like a dormant seed waiting for the right conditions, our counsel will take root. Our words, and the words of so many others, join like a chorus and sing quietly to them in the watches of the night. Sooner or later they will have a close call, a brush with disaster or maybe just a foolish plunge across some self-imposed barrier they thought was firm.

In those sobering moments of reflection, when they lie in their beds at night and stare into the darkness, they will remember and ponder on the words spoken by people who have loved and cared about them…people like you and me. Perhaps at that critical moment they will see with clarity the truth about where their life is headed and cause them to cry out too, "God, please help me change."

I'm also learning that even though I need to talk about the destructive aspects of the party life, the most powerful messengers are fellow students. I once asked a senior, who was behind in credits and attending adult school three nights a week, to come and speak to a class of sophomores who were in deep, academic trouble. Their freshman year GPAs were typically at 1.0, or lower, and if things didn't turn around their sophomore year their chances of graduating would be slim. This older student leaned against the front of my desk and described his normal school day:

- 7:15 a.m. arrive at school; 7:30 a.m. first period begins
- 2:30 p.m. school ends after a full schedule of six classes
- 2:30–4:30 p.m. eat and do homework
- 4:30 p.m. drive across town to night school
- 5:00–9:15 p.m. attend night school
- 10:00 p.m. home (exhausted; more homework)

Why this schedule? Because it was the only way to earn enough credits to graduate on time. As he described his day and how hard it was to keep up with the demands I could see the sophomores listening intently. He went on to describe his night school classmates. Most were court-ordered adults on probation, and in his class of 40 students only a handful were his age. He actually felt scared going to and from his car before and after every class. Some of the older students were in their forties and had committed some pretty ugly crimes.

One sophomore asked him, *"How did you get behind in credits to where you had to go to night school?"* He replied, *"I made some really poor decisions my freshman and sophomore years in school."* I liked her follow-up question, *"Um, could you be a little more specific? What kind of poor decisions?"* He was great. He answered straight and true. *"I got involved with the wrong friends and started partying. My grades really suffered and now I have to do all this work just to graduate."*

He was humble and his message was powerful. It only took a few minutes of class time, but it may have done more to motivate these struggling sophomores than any lesson I could have taught or lecture I would have delivered. Not only did it challenge the young students in my class, but it helped this older student as well. It strengthened his resolve to keep going and finish his education.

Beyond sharing inspirational stories and bringing in guest speakers, there are other things we can do as well that are more closely related to our curriculum. For example, as a biology teacher,

I have to follow a pretty tight calendar to get through the curriculum and be sure my students are prepared for those hallowed standardized tests in the spring, but I have found that there are several places in my curriculum where I can teach my content and speak the truth about the party culture at the same time. For example, I teach a unit on the nervous system and the structure and function of the various types of neurons and electrochemical impulses that are so important in the human body. I love to start the unit by showing mug shots of drug addicts before and after months (or even years) of drug abuse. A quick Internet search for "faces of meth" provides some stark pictures that quickly get the students' attention. This has been a great anticipatory set leading into my unit. Drug abuse can do a lot of damage to the nervous system, so it makes a great hook. I teach about the synapse, the space between neurons (nerve cells), and how electrical impulses stimulate the release of chemicals called neurotransmitters that enter the space and travel across to receptor sites on corresponding nerve fibers. That's how our brain receives sensory input…messages from around the body. Cool stuff! Drugs like cocaine and meth clog the reabsorbing sites, so the neurotransmitters build up in the synapse and stimulate the heck out of certain parts of the brain. The result is quite a euphoric feeling—for a while, but then it wears off and the user experiences a huge crash. What's left is a strong desire to re-experience the euphoria. To make things worse, it doesn't take many highs until the over-stimulated receptor sites become damaged, meaning more and more narcotic is needed to achieve the same high feeling the next time around. The addiction cycle has set in and many teenagers, who thought that a little dabbling would be harmless, find themselves in serious trouble. Their lives spin out of control and everything begins to change. Academic achievement doesn't seem all that important anymore, grades and school attendance drop dramatically and future opportunities are lost forever.

Perhaps your curriculum has a place where you can merge your content with some conversations about the pitfalls of riding the party train. A little education, a few stories (possibly your own) and a testimonial or two can make a huge difference to a teenager about to make some poor decisions.

We have to speak the truth in love. It's a message that may require us to deviate from our curriculum, but teenagers desperately need to hear it…their lives may literally depend on it.

Chapter Nine

Fear: It's Not Safe
At My House

****

For children, going to a doctor's office can be a frightening experience. Bad news and bad things seem to happen at those places. Not even the toys, children's books or lollipops can drive away the anxiety. I remember the feeling in the pit of my stomach when it was my turn to go for a visit. Even checkups were traumatic. Doctors were always dreaming up reasons to administer that most horrible of treatments: the dreaded shot. I was convinced I could hear them thinking, "Yep, he'll need a shot for that." To make matters worse, the shots that really hurt the most were accompanied by the humiliation of having to pull your britches down for some old nurse who inflicted the pain directly in the buttocks. Geez! Just going to the doctor and worrying about experiencing pain could make me so anxious that I felt like crying.

Pain, even just the fear of it, can immobilize a person. The importance of everything else in life diminishes in those moments. Fear doesn't even have to be real, or rational, to have a paralyzing effect. I saw this with my own child. It was back to school time and all students in California were required to have their vaccination against whooping cough in order to be enrolled. As I sat in the doctor's office with my two teenagers, I was surprised to see the fear in my daughter's eyes. She was truly frightened of facing a little, harmless needle. As the nurse prepared the serum, she grabbed my arm and squeezed close to me; her cheek pressed against my shoulder, and then she began to cry. In our house we joke around a lot, but I knew this was no time for humor—she was really scared. I found myself thinking,

> *Pain, even just the fear of it, can immobilize a person.*

"It's just a little shot. How bad can it be?"

But for my daughter, it was pure terror. My son was the braver of the two that day, so he went first. She couldn't watch, but when it was over he gave her some reassurance; he couldn't even feel the needle going in. That eased her fear a bit and the panicked look in her eyes softened for a moment. Nevertheless, when her turn came she buried her head in my shoulder again and braced herself against the certain pain. Tears of relief rolled down her cheeks when it was over. It turned out the dreaded shot didn't hurt at all.

Whether real, or imagined, fear can be all-consuming. Nothing else really matters except finding relief and surviving the moment. For some of the struggling young people we encounter at school, that kind of trauma is a daily occurrence. More children than we care to imagine live in unsafe, violent and abusive homes. They bury their heads and brace themselves for pain on a regular basis. Their home has become like the dreaded doctor's office where bad things and bad news have become normal. As I work with students who struggle academically, I am shocked by how many live in a constant state of fear. Every day is filled with anxiety and concern for their own physical and emotional safety. As the school day draws to an end, they begin to think about what they will face when they get home. For them, home is not a safe place. There are people there who are frightening, and even dangerous.

In this chapter you will hear from some of these students. Try to imagine the feeling in the pit of their stomach and the stress that crawls across their body as they wonder what kind of abuse awaits them when they get home. Preoccupied with friends, classwork, and the routines of school, they can push the anxious feelings to the periphery, but as the day comes to a close, and the time to return home nears, unsettling questions begin to haunt them.

> *What's waiting for me there?*
> *Will there be yelling?*
> *Will there be hitting and shoving?*
> *Which dad will come home from work today?*
> *Will he be sober, or twisted by the effects of alcohol?*
> *Will he be pleasant, or unreasonable and violent?*

Will Mom get slapped around again tonight?

If I hear her scream, should I risk interfering?

Should I call the police this time?

One afternoon I threatened to call home and talk to the parents of a student who had gotten lazy and was falling behind in her schoolwork. Her face and her cheeks flushed bright red and a terrified look crossed her face. Surprised at her reaction, I asked,

"What's going to happen if I call home and tell them how far behind you've fallen in your classes?"

She said softly,

"I'll get beat."

I could see in her eyes that she was telling me the truth, so I switched to plan B and gave her the weekend to catch up on a large amount of work. When Monday came she had completed every assignment. I don't regret threatening to contact her parents, but I'm also glad I didn't make that call. I wonder how many phone calls I've made over the years that led to the abusive treatment of a child. Sometimes it doesn't take much to ignite a fire in an already unstable and flammable environment.

Not long ago I had a senior come and share with my sophomore class about his life. He explained how he coped with the fear of going home. His mother would counsel him and his siblings when they walked in the door from school:

"Now, when your father gets here, don't look him in the eye. Just go to your room and stay there. If he talks to you, don't argue— just do what he says."

The fear was palpable and constant in his house. His mother knew how fragile the peace could be, but she felt powerless to change the situation. She had no means of support for herself and her children without her husband's income. So she stayed, trying to protect them as best she could.

There are some amazing kids sitting in our classrooms. Although they seem pleasant at school, we would be shocked by the kind of violence and stress they face every day at home. It's a wonder some of them function as well as they do. For these students, school is their refuge; it's the safest place in their life. It's where they have friends who accept them and where they feel safe from being hurt.

> *For many students, school is their refuge; it's the safest place in their life.*

For others, the sad reality is, that the problems at home are compounded by additional problems at school. A child unsupported, neglected and abused at home will often feel insecure, lonely and inadequate with peers. The absence of love and security within the family unit often leaves a child ill equipped to make and maintain healthy relationships outside the family. They may lack confidence and find it difficult to trust others. Bracing against pain has become a way of life and getting too close to people has proven dangerous.

Fear and stress at home, and fear and stress at school: for some, it's a double dose of anxiety. And then, of course, there is that English report, the Earth Science exam and that pesky Geometry homework. Some kids just don't have the luxury to worry about school. They have bigger concerns and more immediate traumas to survive.

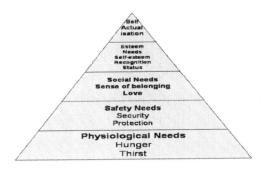

Academic achievement, though important, doesn't hold a candle to the need for safety. It's right there in Maslow's Hierarchy of Needs, right above the need to eat, drink and find shelter. According to Maslow, establishing safety comes before developing self-esteem, which stems from achievement, mastery and recognition. Creativity, the development of talents and true fulfillment (self-actualization) are perched even further up the hierarchy and remain far out of reach for the child in an unstable home.

As you read the following stories, try to understand how fear can be a powerful, hidden "root" that leads to low academic achievement, chronic absenteeism and apathy.

<u>Story #1</u>

For most of my life, I have been struggling with self-esteem issues. I have always been shy and self-conscious in front of people. I quit all of the sports teams I've ever been on. It seems I can never start something and complete it. If I could have had it my way, I would have slept and never woken up, but I know the world does not work like that. Eventually I realized why I was like this.

My mom was 16 when she had me. I was an accident, of course. My dad was a total ass to her. He was always high on heroin and meth, and he'd leave it lying around. He slept all day and, when he wasn't sleeping, he was partying, sleeping with other women, and beating me and my mom. When I was three, my mom divorced my dad. She was sick of him and wanted to raise me in a healthier environment. For the next few years, my dad stayed high a lot. He couldn't keep a job, and was always moving. Somehow, he and my mother, had shared custody, so I had to go to my dad's every other weekend. I would be dropped off at our scheduled time to either find that he wasn't even home, or that he was on heroin and in bed with another woman. On those days when he wasn't home, I was dropped off and had to stay the night outside the front door of his apartment building.

Eventually, after a couple of arrests, my dad promised me he was going to change. I started actually wanting to go to his house, even though my mom hated that I had to. They argued constantly and my dad would sometimes lose his temper in public. They fought over me for custody, each one of them telling me how bad the other was. I never got to have a normal life. I later found out my dad had no intention of changing, and continued doing what he did best: partying, shooting up heroin and selling drugs.

When I was in 3rd grade my mom remarried and we moved in with her new husband. My new stepdad seemed normal enough until one night I walked into the living room and found them arguing. She threatened to call the cops and he told her, "Go ahead." When she reached for the phone, he grabbed her by the throat and started choking her. I ran over and punched him, which didn't help. He swatted me away like nothing. I have no idea what happened then; maybe I've forced myself to forget. The next day, while he was at work, my mom woke me up and told me to pack. We were leaving. We stayed with a friend for a couple of weeks, but my step dad found us and threatened to make our lives a living hell, so we went back home.

By now I no longer trusted anyone. This was the fourth elementary school I had gone to. I had not seen my dad in a year or two because he was in prison. When I went to school, I was constantly picked on and beat up. In 6th grade, I got into a lot of fights. Then, along came junior high. It

> **For the rest of 9th grade I attended community school.**

was hell. I had no friends for most of 7th grade—everyone hated me. I made a fool of myself so much and I continued to get in a few fights. Eighth grade was just as bad.

Finally high school came along, and I was nervous. I only knew a few people. I had decided to be a different person that summer and had started smoking weed a lot. For the first few months of 9th grade I was too high to even focus. From weed came *depression. I spent about a month in a psychiatric hospital because I had tried offing myself. I guess, deep down, I didn't want to die or else I wouldn't be here. When I got out a few weeks later I kept cutting myself, so I was sent to another hospital. Around Christmas my grades started improving, I had made a lot of friends, stopped smoking, stopped wanting to kill myself, had a girlfriend and so on.*

Then I made the stupid mistake one day of going to the PE locker room and stealing stuff out of a kid's locker. It felt really good. I spent his money at Taco Bell for some friends. Somehow, the security guards found out and, the next thing I knew, I was kicked out of school. For the rest of 9th grade I attended community school. I had become so depressed I started smoking weed again. A teacher showed me how to play the guitar. Months went by and I got pretty good. It was the only thing I cared about, the only thing keeping me going.

My dad went to Teen Challenge for a couple of years and we started to be close for the first time. He was actually the one that got me to like playing guitar in the first place.

After my time at community school, I was finally caught up on credits. Sophomore year started and I went to a new school. I hated every second of it. The people annoyed me so much and I couldn't even figure out why. I wanted to punch everyone who walked past me; I wanted to strangle the people in my classes. I wasn't mentally stable enough for school so they switched me to independent studies for half the year. I had grown increasingly bored. Then my mom and I moved again to the other side of town, and that's when I came to this school for the first time. What can I say? I felt almost normal for the first time in so long. I didn't want to punch people, I was actually happy to see people again. I made some friends on my first day, kids who are still my friends now. I was almost happy and mentally healthy—almost.

Summer came and I decided I wanted to learn some responsibility, so I started working for the family business. I worked hard, the hardest I had ever worked. I made a lot of money and felt like I was actually doing something useful. The weeks went by and summer was almost over. I had been making my mom proud of me, hadn't smoked in a long time and I felt really good about myself. I feel like I can do really well this year, my junior year. We'll see. Anyway, this is the story of my life.

After reading this young man's story, I thought I would try to identify some of the major roots that contributed to his academic downfall, but it's complicated. Below are just a few of the things that jumped out at me.

Self-esteem issues, feeling self-conscious, loneliness

I was an accident.

I never had a normal life.

I made a fool of myself so much.

I had no friends for most of 7th grade. Everyone hated me.

Depression

I wanted to sleep and never wake up.

Abuse, violence at home

He grabbed her by the throat and started choking her.

I ran over and punched him. He swatted me away.

Bullied

At school I was constantly picked on and beat up.

Self-destruction

I tried offing myself.

I kept cutting myself.

Drug abuse

I was so depressed, I started smoking weed again.

For the first months of 9th grade I was too high to even focus.

Anger

I wanted to punch everyone who walked past me.

I wanted to strangle the people in my classes.

I got into a lot of fights.

Abandonment

I stayed the night outside the front door of his apartment.

There were times when my dad wasn't even home.

Despite all the storms in this young man's life, something new began to happen, things began to change.

I felt almost normal for the first time in so long.

For those of us who have not suffered so much, or faced so many obstacles, it can be difficult to understand how good it is just to feel normal. Why the breakthrough? Why the corner turned? Was he just maturing and growing up?

I see several things that made the big difference.

- *My dad went to Teen Challenge for a couple of years and we started to be close for the first time.*

  Forgiveness. Healing. Restoration.

- *I made some friends on my first day, kids who are still my friends now.*

  Friendship. Companionship. Acceptance.

- *I started working and I felt like I was actually doing something useful.*

  Becoming productive and useful. Having worth.

- *I had been making my mom proud of me.*

  Praise. Affirmation. Being acknowledged.

- *I hadn't smoked in a long time.*

  Self-respect. Self-discipline. Freedom.

- *I felt really good about myself.*

  Peace. Wholeness. Self-esteem.

- *I feel like I can do really well this year.*

  Hope!

This young man is not out of the woods yet, but he is well on his way to overcoming some pretty big storms in his life. I believe that writing his story and sharing it with a caring adult has been a part of the healing process. He took a risk, wrote down the struggles he'd faced in his life and then he shared them with another person. As a result, a connection was made. He and I have a little history now. I know a piece of him that most people don't know and his secrets are safe. I asked if I could share his story in this book and he gave me permission.

Most mornings he gets a ride to school with a friend, but they must drop him off twenty minutes early. Many of those mornings he comes to my classroom and sits on my couch. If it's a cold morning I'll let him heat some water in the microwave and make hot chocolate before the school day begins. Sometimes he does homework; other times he's on the phone texting a friend. Over time we've accrued a solid balance of "relational equity," the kind we discussed in chapter three.

One day I had to make a withdrawal of sorts. He was letting some schoolwork slip, getting a little lazy—typical teenage stuff. I had to get a little blunt with him and serve up some straight talk about responsibility, but he took it well—a little defensiveness, but none of his typical defiance. There was no rolling of the eyes or tuning out. He knew he deserved it, and our relationship could handle a little confrontation. In the past there might have been an explosion, but not today.

"I see a big difference in you this year," I said during one of our casual conversations.

"What's that?"

"You seem happy." He smiled, nodded his head and said, "Yea, I am".

Story #2

My family is not really that good. When I turned five that was the first time my dad hit my mom and me. My dad continued doing this until me and my mom moved out when I was 15. My mom started doing really well. We had an apartment down by the east side. One day my mom left for work and never came back. I ended up going and living with my grandma. I haven't seen my dad or my mom in over a year. I really don't plan on seeing my mom, but eventually I do want to see my dad again. I've been living with my grandma for four months so far. I've been doing way better with her. It's like a real family that I could always count on to be there for me when I really need them. I don't plan on moving out until I'm old enough to be on my own. To be honest, I still miss my parents very much. I don't understand why I got put into a family like mine. I guess that's just another question I'll never know the answer to."

Ten years of physical abuse at his father's hand, but I wonder what hurt worse: being hit, or watching his mom take the blows? After so much strife and pain, his mom finally rescued him from the violence. They moved out and left the abuser. Then the unthinkable happens…his mom serves up some abuse of her own. Security, self-worth, significance and trust all disappear in a moment.

"One day, my mom left for work and never came back."

Abandonment—it's perhaps the ultimate abuse. Who could discard a child? To do so sends a horrible and unmistakable message:

You are not important to me.

I don't want you.

I don't need you.

I don't even love you enough to care what happens to you.

It's no surprise this young man is left confused.

120

"I don't understand why I got put into a family like mine."

It will take a lot of support, affirmation and love to convince this teenager that his mom was wrong about him.

Story #3

My father drank more and more each week. He would come home later and later. My mom was left to raise us by herself. As time went by, my dad started physically and verbally abusing my mom. I was being bullied at school, and then, at home I waited for night to come. That's when my dad would hit my mom. It was tough.

My dad decided to move away for a few months when I was in 5th grade. When he came back he brought this map of a new place to live. He said he was changing his ways and wanted us to start with a clean slate by moving us to a new town. It was awesome! I went to a great school and my mom got a job. My dad...well, he didn't have a job. A few months went by and we were back to where we started; dad coming home at 9 or 10 at night, drinking an entire 36-pack, and me hearing my mom two doors down: her cries and screams. To make matters worse, a few months into my 5th grade year my dad started abusing me. By the time I turned 11, my dad was hitting me daily. But he wasn't the only one abusing me. My grandmother, his mother, was abusing me too. I don't think I've ever heard a compliment from her. She told me if I was fat no one would want to marry me and then I would fail at life. She told me my mom was crazy and my dad was too good for her. My dad's family would also tell me bad things about my mom; how fat, stupid and crazy she was. I heard these things every holiday, celebration and reunion. I knew it wasn't true. I also figured they didn't know about the physical abuse.

> **School was my haven. It was where I was safe from my dad's swings, my grandmother's words and from seeing my mom's bruises.**

School was my haven. It was where I was safe from my dad's swings, my grandmother's words and from seeing my mom's bruises. When I entered 6th grade I was at my lowest point. One night, two weeks after school started, everything got out of hand. It all happened so fast. To sum it up, my dad had beat up my mom to the point where she was vomiting blood and he severely physically abused my brothers and me. I called the police and my dad was later found and arrested near our house. From there, my mom, my brothers and I were all granted a restraining order from my dad.

After 6 months my dad got in contact with my mom. He begged and pleaded and promised he'd changed this time. So we went back, but of course the alcohol would win my dad over again. He became violent at all hours of the day, even abusing my mother and me when he was sober. That was the scary part. He would give the occasional hit to my brothers, but not as bad as he did to my mom. She wasn't allowed to have friends, wear her hair a certain way, watch certain things on TV, or listen to certain music. Life went into a downward spiral. Soon my family had lost everything, even our car and our home.

With no income, we moved in to a 3-bedroom apartment. We went from living in a quiet neighborhood in a nice house, to a place where a lot of the families were on welfare. That was a big culture shock. After 2 weeks my dad had enough. He packed his bags and told me I would be on drugs and never amount to anything because he wasn't going to be in my life. That was the last time he lived with us. The next time I saw him was a year later when my parents got divorced.

Once my dad was out of my life things seemed happier. My mom regained a lot of confidence. I started seeing her laugh more often, and to make this story even better, we found Jesus. I'm not saying my life is perfect now. My mom still struggles, but not in the way we used to. Money is tight, we're on welfare, and we're still going through the healing process. It helped a lot when I got a transfer to come to this school because now I live at my best friend's house most of the time. Her parents and siblings are like family and it helps my mom; she doesn't need to drive back and forth every day.

In high school I did have a hiccup with my grades, but I'm back on track now and I have set some goals in life. I want to succeed and spread the love God has given me. I have forgiven my dad for all he has done in a letter I have written him. I see him every now and then, but I still keep my guard up.

It seems that often in tandem with drug and alcohol abuse comes violence. When under the influence, an agitated and unhappy parent can quickly lose restraint and become dangerous. The violent episodes usually escalate over time until an incident spirals out of control, often requiring the police to get involved.

The violence in this young girl's family led to a severely disrupted lifestyle. Literally overnight everything changed and she went from affluence to poverty. The word "shock" sums it up pretty well. Sadly, the removal of a parent from the family was the beginning of restored stability and peace at home.

Once my dad was out of my life, things seemed happier.

The hardest thing about writing this chapter was not finding stories that fit the topic, but trying decide which to include.

There were so many.

Along with the devastation of divorce and the beckoning of friends to join them on the party train, students struggling in school often echo the confession:

It's not safe at my house.

We can't underestimate how difficult it is for students to focus on their education when they live in an atmosphere of fear. The primal instinct to survive supersedes the desire to learn and develop intellectually.

Is there anything we can do to help these kids?

Yes! We can make school as safe a place as possible; a place of refuge where there is no fear of physical or emotional harm. We won't always know which of our students come from violent homes therefore we must be cautious. For the student from a home of where violence and abuse are common, even a raised tone of voice can be extremely upsetting. The same primal instincts to fight or flee that a student relies upon for survival at home can be inadvertently stimulated by a teacher conveying a demeaning or aggressive tone in the classroom.

Imagine for a moment a pit bull, charging across the street toward you. Suddenly you are perched on the hood of a minivan wondering how in the world you got up there. When faced with danger we all instinctively prepare to run for cover, but if fleeing doesn't promise safety, we resort to plan B...combat. Students can react in similar ways emotionally when they perceive themselves in a threatening situation. Demeaning comments, for example, from a frustrated teacher, can feel just like the verbal abuse from an angry parent. It's familiar territory. To "survive" they may attempt to "flee" by pulling away and becoming sullen, silent and inattentive...withdrawal. If that doesn't prove effective they may resort to "combat" and become aggressive, argumentative and defiant. Both reactions come from the primal need to survive, and during these episodes, learning and intellectual development will invariably take a backseat. This is why a calm, quiet and non-threatening learning atmosphere can be extremely helpful for students who come from stressful, unsafe homes.

We can provide that. We can avoid the use of putdowns, demeaning comments and insulting remarks. When a student becomes argumentative, we can refuse to engage in the verbal sparring that hurts feelings and often escalates into angry outbursts. Of course we cannot always avoid conflict. We will inevitably need to enforce rules and administer consequences for inappropriate behavior, but in doing so, we can maintain our professionalism and avoid the temptation to assault the dignity of a student we are upset with. We are the adult in the room…we can't forget that, and we must not allow ourselves to be pulled down into a verbal exchange that becomes personal and hurtful.

> *Demeaning comments from a frustrated teacher can feel just like the verbal abuse from an angry parent.*

Students from unsafe homes probably don't look forward to school because they love Biology, Math or English, but because school is a safe and peaceful place: a place where they are not afraid. The less threatened they feel, the freer they become to learn, and for some, the most helpful thing we can do is simply provide a calm place where they can get their homework done.

Years ago, while teaching at a junior high, I was having a conversation with a colleague in the teachers' workroom. I listened quietly to his ranting as he described how ignorant and pathetic his students were. According to him they lacked intelligence and were disrespectful little monsters. The more he vented, the more agitated I became. Ironically, I was teaching those same kids in my Life

126

Science class and I loved them. I could see the real problem was the way he perceived his students. They had picked up on his disdain for them, and so they set out to make his life a living hell in return. Being new to the profession, and this man my senior, I held my tongue...for a while, but when he referred to the kids as "little a**holes," I couldn't take it anymore. I got angry. I turned away from the copy machine, faced him, and said, "Stop! That's enough. Calling kids names like that is unprofessional and offensive. If you hate teaching that much, then please do the profession a favor and get out."

Well, that shut him up. Later he apologize for his rant, but unfortunately, I doubt his attitude toward his students changed much. He was a man in a profession he didn't enjoy and teaching Math had become a way to get a paycheck. Teachers who have become cynical, and have lost their love for children, can become emotionally dangerous. They forget they are not teaching a subject: they are teaching people; some of whom are wounded and fragile. Every school has a few teachers, I suppose, who have lost their sensitivity; who are more concerned about having an easy day at work than touching lives and making a difference.

We all have a bad day now then, and sometimes we may even need to vent our frustrations, but when bad days turn into bad weeks, and bad months, we're in trouble...and so are the students we are there to help. We are in a people-helping profession, and if we become impatient, quick-tempered and cynical, it's time to do some soul searching. We can't become another abusive adult in the lives of young people. We have to find a way back to our first love as educators—or find another way to make a living.

Some students will tell us, "It's not safe at my house" but they should never say, "It's not safe at my school." Though we can't remove all the baggage that students bring to school or control what happens when the bell rings at the end of the day, we can make school a safe place, a place of refuge where dreams have a real shot at coming true.

Chapter Ten

Death: There's a Hole in my Heart

****

When grandpa died it felt like there was a weight inside of my chest. It was hard to move, or even breathe. It felt like something huge was missing.

****

Grief is an empty, lost feeling. When I feel grief I just want to sleep forever. It's a lonely, longing feeling that comes over my body and I start to shake. A single word can set me off; even a touch from the wrong person can make me want to cry.

I really don't know if I can write this chapter. I'm certainly not qualified and I am profoundly aware that I'm in water way over my head; but I can't leave this chapter out either.

I know I won't be able to capture in words, with any precision, how it feels to grieve the loss of someone loved. I will fall desperately short because grief feels so different for each of its victims. Some who've lost a person close to them might say, "You nailed it; that's just how I felt." Someone else might say, "You haven't the slightest clue what it's really like."

My purpose here is not to out-do the great writers and poets of the world who have eloquently written about loss, but only to remind us that sometimes students appear apathetic and uncaring about school because they're lost in a dark empty place with no light…or escape…or hope of relief: a place called grief.

Many years ago, when I was teaching in a junior high, my students were cleaning cages and feeding animals in my after school Critter Club. One of the regulars was a shy boy who rarely attracted attention to himself. He seemed to love animals and my old shop class converted to science lab was full of all sorts of interesting creatures. If it were not for his involvement in the Critter Club I might not have noticed him in class where he usually sat quietly, did his work quietly, and when the bell rang at the end of the period…left quietly. But on this day I noticed him. With all the animals cared for and the chores done for the day, we sat for a few minutes and fed romaine lettuce to some grateful guinea pigs. As the little fur balls squealed and munched on their snack, our casual conversation turned to family.

What do your parents do?" I asked. His reply,

"My mom passed away six months ago."

That was an answer I didn't expect, and immediately I felt a tightening in my chest. I was not only stunned, but I felt ashamed.

His mother had been lost in the first weeks of school and I had been completely unaware.

How did I miss it?

The realization that one of my students had been dealing with that kind of loss and grief, without my knowledge, was unnerving. I went home that night troubled. I scanned my memories, hoping I hadn't been stern or hard on him during those agonizing days and weeks of grief. I wondered: Did I snap at him for sleeping in class? Was I short with him for not paying attention? Did I show frustration and exasperation for his missing work or repeated absences? Had I trampled on his already broken heart in some unintentional way? I felt so sorry for him, and so disappointed in myself for being completely clueless.

In education we often scan across the faces of several hundred students in a day, yet never really see them. They mill through our classrooms like cattle grazing through a meadow. Some are playful and loud; others quietly forage and move on. We give most of our attention to the spunky ones that seem more intent on playing than "eating" what we have to offer. The quiet grazers, on the other hand, are often overlooked. They're the loners, the daydreamers, the ones who miss a lot of school, and when they do show up, they don't seem very interested in learning. Their name bleeps across our radar at report card time because they're missing work and their grades are low. We might not like to admit it, but we make a lot of assumptions about underachievers. We have them pegged as lazy and apathetic, but sometimes we are horribly mistaken. Sometimes our wrong assumptions are a much bigger problem than their poor achievement.

It's so important that we ask questions and probe a little when we have a student who is "present"…but absent. We have to look deeper when we notice their heads are down and they seem detached and unconcerned about learning. The most important thing we can do with a student who is disengaged and withdrawn is invest some time, build some trust and find out their story!

Sometimes I get tunnel vision and miss the glaringly obvious. Swept up in the grand mission to prepare students for the real world…for life, college, and coveted Benchmark exams and Standardized State Tests, I lose perspective. I fall into the trap of seeing student achievement as a reflection of my effectiveness as a teacher and the underperforming student becomes a frustration. With that subtle change in focus, from their needs to mine, I can come across stern and even demeaning. And then one day it happens. I'm jolted out of my tunnel by an unexpected revelation that the unmotivated, apathetic underachiever I've been hounding all semester has been desperately treading water in the deep end of life, and I didn't see it. When they needed a life preserver and a way to safety, I was pushing their head under, and in not so many words, telling them, "Swim, you lazy kid."

What a horrible feeling it is to learn that a child I've harshly admonished has been living through a traumatic situation and I made it even worse. Sometimes the discovery doesn't come until they disappear from school and I ask other students about them. It makes me sigh when I hear the reply, "Oh, his mom died three months ago and he went to live with his grandparents." That's when the dart goes in and stabs me in the heart. That's when I know I really blew it.

In other cases there might be some kind of breakdown at school that reveals the trauma. I saw this graphically played out in my General Studies class one day. There are two computers near my desk in the front of the room, and that day a young lady was sitting at one of them writing her life story; a story that included the death of her dear mother. Nearly a year and a half had passed since the loss of her mom but she was still defenseless against the pangs of grief. The

> *"Sometimes grief feels like a ghost that will haunt you for the rest of your life."*

class was working quietly on their assignments when suddenly she burst into tears and ran from the room. The rest of us were taken by surprise. None of us knew what precipitated her outburst, but I could see right away the class expected me to investigate. I couldn't just sit there and ignore this distressed young lady, so after a few seconds of pondering, I did something a little unorthodox...I breached teacher protocol, left the classroom and went looking for her. Fortunately I didn't have to go very far. She was just outside my room sitting on a bench, sobbing uncontrollably. Well, that led to another breach of protocol. I sat down beside her, put my arm around her heaving shoulders, held her tight and let her cry.

Eventually she was able to express what was happening. That day in class, as she was writing her story, she found herself remembering the final week of her mother's life and the horrible sounds she made while struggling to breathe. The vivid memories came back and grief swept down like an avalanche and buried her alive. Sometimes the pain of losing someone takes a long time to go away. And, as another student wrote,

"Sometimes grief feels like a ghost that will haunt you for the rest of your life."

There are reminders of that absent person at every turn and just the right (or wrong) memory can trigger the sadness all over again.

A few days later this hurting young lady finished her story.

Last year my mother passed away...about 16 months now to be exact. It's been pretty painful. I now live alone with my dad. She developed breast cancer about 7 years ago that gradually turned into bone cancer and then finally liver cancer. That's when it really started going downhill. After it moved to her liver it was only a week that she suffered. It was absolutely the worst feeling ever, just knowing that it was the last week with her, and soon, I would never see her again. We tried to make it memorable and make the best of it. We were all the sweetest and the most caring we could be. The doctors had told us abruptly one day that she was being taken off all her medication and pain killers because it was useless; she wasn't going to last much longer. That upset us quite a bit, but the doctor was sadly right; nothing would help her to feel any better except just straight morphine. Soon she was checked into hospice because she was beginning to fade and all the collected chemicals from her liver started to build up and cloud her mind so she couldn't talk, walk, or even function correctly. For her limited time remaining with us she had to be put in a hospital bed set in the front room by the couch and hooked up to an oxygen machine to assist her breathing. As all her organs slowly shut down over the remaining week I can just remember the look on my dad's face as he constantly stared at her teary eyed from over the side rail of the bed. He would look at me and tell me to hold his hand as he hid his face in his other hand. I would just sit there in denial telling myself that everything was going to be ok and that she would get over it, but I was soon proven wrong. Her lungs soon started to shut down, which forced her to utter a horrible noise that sounded like she was drowning in her own body with each breath that she took in and out. Still to this day, I hear that wretched noise in the back of my mind; shallow, crackly, hollow and short. I try to shut it out, but it still haunts me.

> **Nearly a year and a half had passed since the loss of her mom, but she was still defenseless against the pangs of grief.**

There is no way to describe it to anyone because no one could ever fathom how it curled your spine and made your heart drop. I remember her struggling to speak and the faces that she made as she tried to mouth out short sentences. At one point I specifically recall her trying to say something with all of her might because she was grunting, looking at me intently and gasping for extra air as if about to scream, so my dad leaned his head down close to her face and stared at her lips to try and recognize what she was saying. He then turned to me with tear filled eyes and told me, "She said I love you baby." That got to me and I started to tear up; and then I leaned over and gave her a kiss on the cheek, accidentally dropping tears on her forehead. She smiled and looked at me as if trying to tell me something through her eyes. I understood completely and gave her a hug and told her I loved her with all my heart and that I would never ever stop loving her. Her eyes began to water and a single tear streamed down her cheek; I caught it with my finger.

That last week we had to feed her and give her water through a straw. We gave her our full attention for three or four days straight and then I remember being woken up by my dad crying and shaking me saying, "Wake up, she's passing!" I got up and ran out to the front room to find my dad and a hospice nurse gathered around the bed with my mom's head stuck in one direction facing the fireplace. She was breathing really shallow and slow. We immediately said we loved her, and a few seconds later her face went blank, and then her eyes relaxed, along with her eyebrows. Her mouth dropped open a little and that's when she stopped breathing. The nurse tried to shut her eyes, but they wouldn't close, as if they were fighting to stay open to see everything, and stay with us in this life, but she was already too far gone for it to matter. The next thing I remember is just falling to the floor; slumping over in silence as my dad touched her hair. Two men came in also from Hospice and began to wrap her up in her favorite robe that we had previously gotten her a few years ago for Christmas. They pulled her off the hospital bed to another platform to take her away. I remember jumping up with tears in my eyes and hugging her one last time. I leaned over close to her and told her I loved her and that I was sorry if I was ever bad to her. Then I kissed her...she already felt cold. My dad told me to cut a piece of her hair for a remnant of her, but I couldn't bring myself to desecrate her in such a manner, so my dad had to take the scissors from my hand and do it himself. As soon as I heard the clip of the scissors I ran to the bathroom and locked myself away for hours. I sat against the door blocking everything else out; just thinking how she wouldn't be with me to buy my first car, meet my future husband, help me pick out my special wedding dress or, most of all, to grow old with me and see her own grand babies.

> *"We immediately said we loved her, and a few seconds later her face went blank, and then her eyes relaxed, along with her eyebrows."*

In those days I felt so hollow and ashamed because I realized how horrible I had been to her; how I gave her attitude, was so rude and how I was embarrassed to even take her to a simple football game because she was goofy and a bit weird. Now I realize that it was the biggest mistake and that I was so insensitive. I inherited those wonderful traits from her and it is nothing to be embarrassed *by. She was the best mother in the world and the sweetest, strongest and most loving woman imaginable. I was just to ignorant to realize how great she was and what an honest to God blessing it was to have her in my life, if even for only fifteen short years.*

Sometimes I wish everything would just break away and crumble; just shatter. I wish I was weak so I could finally let go and let out the emotions that I so desperately want to release, but I can't. I somehow won't allow myself. I know it sounds like insanity, but I sometimes think to myself...begging my mind to let go, begging to cry or to just do anything to ease my mind, but I can't. Sometimes I wish I were weak spirited, in hopes of exhaling some of this stress, but I can't do that either. You may think that it made me so much stronger; that I gained some sort of a defense towards those types of situations and feelings, when honestly, I just feel like I'm in a black hole. It's a sinking feeling. I never shed a tear, or even let myself think of the past, in the fear that I might sadden myself beyond any chance of return. I want to stay happy for her so that when she looks down on me from heaven she will be proud of her little girl and have a smile on her face.

Over the years I've read a lot of student stories, but I don't think I've ever read one that captured, so vividly in words, the raw emotion of losing a loved one. As articulate and gifted a writer as this young lady is, she was failing every class, and eventually had to attend an alternative high school.

Until recently it had not occurred to me how many of our students will lose a loved one during their school age years; a grandparent, an uncle, an aunt, a friend…maybe even a parent or a sibling. That loss will likely rock their world for a while. Most will be ill-equipped and unprepared for the grief they will find themselves struggling through. The primary elixir for their pain will be time, but what will happen to them academically while the elixir does the slow work of healing?

When death comes knocking, and someone close is snatched away forever, school may not feel all that important.

I'm not sure there is a very useful manual for helping students floundering through a season of grief, but I do know this; I never want to blow it again and misinterpret grief and assume it was apathy. They look a lot the same, but there is a big difference. Apathy declares, "I *don't* care about school," while grief whispers, "I *can't* handle school…not right now."

The apathetic student often appears lazy an unmotivated, so we prod and push them to snap out of their doldrums. We give them what apathy often requires…tough love and straight talk. We don't pull any punches or sugar coat reality. Instead we tell them the truth and hope our frankness will jolt them out of their unmotivated stupor. When we deal with apathetic students we can't be enablers. Caring has to include accountability because it doesn't really help when we coddle teenagers who make poor choices and behave inappropriately. Sometimes positive changes won't happen without conflict, and anyone who has worked with at-risk students knows the road to growth and progress can be a bumpy ride. But if we mis-diagnose the situation and think that what we're seeing is apathy, when in fact it is grief, we may prescribe a treatment that compounds the problem.

Untimely tough love is not helpful to an already overwhelmed and grieving teenager. For those special circumstances, when tragedy strikes close to home, the appropriate response is comfort, not confrontation; empathy and understanding, not a lecture on "It's time to grow up and be responsible."

I shudder to think how many times I've been tough on a kid when I didn't know the whole story. I'm sure we've all been guilty at one time or another; we just didn't know.

How could we?

To avoid making that mistake I'm learning to do a few simple things. I'm asking more questions and probing a little more before I make assumptions. I'm calling students to my desk more often than I used to and inquiring,

"Are you okay?"

"You seem down and disconnected; is everything all right?"

I find kids usually respond honestly to questions like that, especially if they believe you really care about them.

Fortunately, the lack of motivation in most apathetic students is not caused by the trauma of losing a loved one. But when, as one student wrote, *"grief feels like a weight inside my chest,"* we can't afford to be horribly wrong.

Chapter Eleven

Moving: Lessons from Clara

****

A few short summers ago, while on vacation with my family in Oregon, I learned about Clara. Her origins and background were a bit of a mystery, but one thing was obvious…she was beautiful. She had found her way to my parents little ranch and my loving mother took her in. There was always room for one more; my mom could never resist a wayward soul. You have to remember, she's the woman who hand fed literally dozens of orphaned lambs in dead of winter and (as ranch midwife) gave mouth-to-snout recitation to a newborn piglet until he squealed his own first breath. She's the lady that set up a hospice in the old ranch house and cared for two aging mothers, her own and my dad's, so they could live out their final days with dignity. And we must not forget, she's also the woman, along with my father, who took in and loved over ninety foster children over the years; giving them a place to call home. So it didn't surprise me about Clara. She needed some tender love and a place to set her roots down. The old ranch was the perfect place.

By the time I saw Clara she had been under my mother's gentle hand for quite some time and was doing very well. I'm a little embarrassed to admit it now, but I confess; when I saw Clara, I had this odd compulsion to take her home…to have her for myself. Though I have several of my own, I wanted Clara too, and to my delight, my wife agreed.

Clara's full name is *Clerodendrum thomsoniae,* and her family originated in West Africa. Being a deciduous creature, my Clara loses her foliage every winter, but come spring, new leaves appear like outstretched hands with white and red blossoms filling every branch. Some have nick named her "Bleeding Heart Vine" while others refer to her as "Glory Bower", but no matter what you call her, she faithfully produces the same amazing aroma every summer; it's a scent that permeates the back yard like a sweet perfume.

It's been nearly 8 years now and Clara stands twenty feet tall and fills the corner of the yard. I'm also happy to announce, she's not alone. Every spring a brood of runners pop up around her feet, and being an amateur landscaper, I love to pluck a few and strategically plant them around the yard to fill gaps and provide shade.

This past year, however, I made a grave mistake; one I will not make again. One of Clara's "children" was growing quite well near the patio. It was only about six feet tall, but full of leaves and on its way to becoming a suitable companion for my fruitless mulberry and smoke plum tree. But there was a problem…I needed to move Clara's child to make room for three new date palms that required that space. It shouldn't have been a big deal. I simply had to move the juvenile across the yard. Being a Biology teacher, and bit of a botanist, I knew August was not the best time for the procedure, but it had to be done. So with great care, I dug up all the soil in a two foot radius around Clara's child, making sure none of the roots were severed by my shovel. I then carefully placed the transplant in a newly dug hole and gently surrounded it with potting soil; adding lots of water and a bit of fertilizer. I was sure the extraction and removal would have little, if any impact. I fully expected the juvenile shrub to take root in its new location and live happily ever after.

Boy, was I wrong!

The very next morning I went out to inspect the yard, as I am accustomed to doing in the lazy months of summer, and to my surprise, Clara's child looked horribly ill. The leaves were completely wilted; drooping like the ears on a forlorn dog. Compared to its sibling fifteen feet due west, the shrub appeared on the brink of death.

"What in the world had happened?" I thought.

How could it be in such a terrible state when I took great care in its moving?

I was perplexed.

In the days that followed I watched helplessly as all the leaves fell to the ground, leaving only naked branches in their place. There had been ample water and lots of sun, but it was clear… there was no hope. I considered pulling up the naked tree, but decided instead to wait. Perhaps some thread of life might lay dormant in what was left.

A full year passed before I saw leaves again. Ironically, the tree fifteen feet away had grown tremendously. It was a full three feet taller with three times the foliage. The juvenile tree had experienced what more veteran landscapers refer to as transplant shock. Having been disrupted, the roots had trouble nourishing the leaves with sufficient water, so they wilted and fell to the ground. The naked stem that remained held on to life by a thread.

Hmm! Why am I telling this story in a book for educators trying to help apathetic students?

Well, I've thought a lot about Clara and her offspring as I work with challenging students. The motivation and desire to achieve academically has "wilted" in many of them, and as I try to understand the "roots" of their apathy, I've noticed a reoccurring pattern often described in their stories and expressed in the statement…

"And then we moved again!"

Like my Clarodendrum, being uprooted and relocated shocks a child in ways we might never expect. Frequent moving, for whatever the reason, makes it very difficult for those transplanted to establish their roots, to stabilize and to blossom. The shock of relocation can be so disturbing that it can require months to recover.

It's true for shrubs…and it's true for kids.

Let's take a look at a few of their stories and crawl into their teenage skin for a moment. Try to understand why "moving again" can be so difficult and cause such a setback to academic success.

I have been to twelve different schools in the course of eleven years. Third grade was the year I started switching schools due to personal life issues. I think I went to about four different schools that year. In fourth grade <u>we moved again</u>. The huge thing on the playground that year was double-dutch jump rope. If you knew how to do that, you were hot stuff. In the fifth grade <u>my family moved</u> to the beach for a short time. At the end of the fifth grade <u>we moved back</u> where we came from. By the time I reached eighth grade my grades had started slipping. Due to family complications and extensive amounts of absences I got behind and I just didn't care.

When <u>I went to live with my mom</u> I was just starting 6th grade. I was scared because it was a new place and I didn't know anyone. Even though I didn't know people I still managed to get good grades and stay out of trouble. <u>Then we had to move</u> in the middle of my 7th grade year. I had another new school to go to and new friends to make. I was terrified because I didn't know how these people would treat me. When I started high school <u>I moved</u> in with my aunt but before the year was over <u>I moved back</u> in with my mom. Over the summer my mom and I started arguing again...we never got along. That's when her boyfriend started getting into our fights and making them worse. My mom and he like to fight a lot too. My mom likes to drink a lot and that makes things a little worse. When 10th grade came I just gave up. I was just so tired of it all. I was *depressed and had anxiety when I was around a lot of people; I still do. Soon I started ditching school, my grades were in the drain and I was on my fourth truancy step. My mom's boyfriend and I got in a fight after I wouldn't tell him what my counselor had talked to me about, so he got mad and told me that I had to move out over the summer. We never talked again after that because he told me I was going to be worthless like my family. My mom didn't even argue with him about it. Its summer time and I've messed up so much I'm in summer school. Just yesterday my mom kicked me out and I had to miss school because I had to find a place to live. I'm living with my aunt again and hoping that I can get through high school. So, I have just one thing left to say... What's going to happen in my life now?*

Transplant shock! I can't imagine twelve schools in eleven years. That kind of repeated disruption is bound to result in a bumpy ride on the path to a good education. She doesn't give a lot of details about why so many moves occurred, but simply indicates *"personal life issues"* and *"family complications."* There was also alcohol, mom's live in boyfriend and a lot of arguing; but what jumps out at me the most are the emotions stirred up in all the moving. This is where I believe adults who work with apathetic teenagers often miss the obvious. We forget what it's like to be thrust into a strange new environment, among strange new people, at the age of 15. Were we mature enough at that age to handle that kind of turbulence? For most teenagers repeated moves are very difficult. We see the outward signs, but often miss the profound effects of the reoccurring cycle of displacement.

"I was scared...I didn't know anyone."

"I was terrified...another new school, new friends to make. How would they treat me?"

By the time a transient student gets to us they have been through transplant shock numerous times. They seem almost numb to the fact they don't have any close friends. There is no one to walk to class with, or to eat lunch with, or to hang out with after school. When the weekend rolls around they sit home alone. Loneliness has become normal; being "wilted" a familiar condition. Some students resist making the effort to sink down roots and make our school their home. Why? Because they have resigned to the likelihood that we will be just another stop in their transient school experience. Repeated moves through elementary and middle school leave their academic scars and by the time they get to high school they often have an atrocious attendance record and big gaps in their learning. Basic skills in Math and English are often missing, along with the disciplines and study skills required to be successful in school. As the assignments get more difficult, they fall further behind. It's heartbreaking, but these students know they are in trouble. They will be the first to tell you, "I'm not very good at school."

"My grades started slipping...I had excessive absences...I got behind."

Eventually, that familiar dark cloud of apathy settles in and discouragement follows. Like a sinister fog, hopelessness creeps in and these kids start giving up on school.

"I just didn't care, I just gave up, I was just so tired of it all."

"I started ditching, I was on my 4th truancy step, my grades were in the drain."

"So, I have just one thing left to say...What's going to happen in my life now?"

It is difficult, and very frustrating, to help students that move a lot. They are usually smitten with the plagued by absenteeism. We invest a lot of time trying to keep them caught up; and then they disappear again. Sadly, some of our most needy students have been like yoyos dropped in one school after another. In their eyes, the most immediate problem is not school, it's establishing friendships, fitting in...belonging.

"I've had a lot of cool friends and <u>lost them from changing schools</u>. I have been to 4 different elementary schools and I am on my third high school. I have a lot of friends at the school I'm at now and I like the teachers. <u>I hope to stay here</u> for the next two years. Friends are all I basically have. Without them I really don't know what I would do. Friends are honestly everything."

More terrifying than trying to make new friends is the prospect of losing the ones that were finally made after at the last move. So why do people move so much?

Breakup of the family?

Job changes?

Poverty...eviction, can't pay rent, moving in with friends and family?

Dysfunction, violence at home, moving to safety?

One student put it this way:

"We never had a lot of money when I was younger. We lived on welfare and we moved whenever we couldn't pay the rent. By the time I was 8 I had lived in 11 different places, including 2 shelters."

Another wrote:

"In first grade it was okay, but a little challenging getting used to the school experience and the new class, <u>but then I moved,</u> so that really sucked. I spent the rest of my first grade year at a new school. My second grade year kind of wasn't a good year because my teacher and I didn't get along at all, so second grade really sucked too. In third <u>grade I ended up moving again because we got evicted,</u> so we moved in with my grandmother, all the way across town, and I <u>had to get used to change once again.</u> In third grade my teacher didn't really understand that I was <u>going through stuff at home, like moving, and I felt alone.</u> And then in fourth grade, I <u>moved again.</u>

I went to middle school, and it kind of sucked because my grade was the youngest grade in the school, but I loved sixth grade. I was doing well academically and I was dating the most popular sixth grader in school. In the seventh grade I had a down fall because <u>my family and I got evicted again.</u>

In the summer of my freshman year <u>I moved</u> to a different high school and <u>I was so mad, because I didn't know anyone.</u>

"Getting used to change"

"Not knowing anyone"

"Feeling alone"

That pretty well describes the plight of the student who has moved a lot. The insecurity of their circumstances is haunting and the gnawing sense of academic doom always looms large. Even hard work may never be enough to make a difference.

We've all had students we enjoyed having in class, but the plague of poor attendance was just too much to overcome. We work hard to help them, but they simply disappear one day and we never hear from them again.

The transient nature of life for these students is very disruptive. Their success in school will always be in jeopardy. Unfortunately, educators don't have much control over this variable, and sadly, neither do they.

For these students I would offer this encouragement...love them as though your school were their last stop. Those who "move a lot" may be caught in a lifestyle that isn't favorable to academic achievement, but they still have incredible value and worth as human beings.

While they are with you be intentional in communicating that truth to them. Your love may be the most important influence keeping them from giving up during this difficult chapter in their life, the chapter where they move a lot.

Chapter Twelve

Not Yet

****

I have talked a lot in the preceding chapters about the unmotivated teenagers who sit in our classrooms; the ones who don't seem to care if they pass or fail and seem content to lay their heads down on their desks and take their "F" quietly. Some of them don't give us much trouble as long as we leave them alone.

But what do we do with them?

Of course, they probably have a story, but we have content to teach, and quite frankly, dealing with the personal drama in a student's life doesn't always fit very well into the typical lesson plan. Some days we may feel like the best we can do is send them to someone else; someone who has time and training to deal with their situation. Maybe the Dean of Students can wake them up, or perhaps a counselor can spark some life into them. With class sizes of 35-40, like we see in many schools today, the needs of the apathetic student becomes very difficult to meet.

This is a big dilemma for the caring teacher trying to make a difference. Probing beneath the surface and learning a student's story can have a significant impact, but it's very time consuming. If you teach a core subject in a regular classroom you're probably doing well to give extra attention to one "sleeper" in each period. Even when we carve out that kind of time, and make that kind of effort, there will still be some students who we just can't seem to reach. Some of the most challenging ones are simply not ready to accept help or make changes. I suppose there will always be students who just don't seem to care about school and despite all our efforts, they may still fail our class.

That's been hard for me to accept, and I know many of you feel the same way. So what do we do with those we can't seem to reach right now? How do we handle the ones who seem determine to "crawl" through the cracks?

I'd like to offer a word of encouragement.

Do the best you can one day at a time, and be at peace with that. Strive to be patient, and never give up believing that even the most apathetic student, at some point down the road, may be ready to change. A summer passes, a new school year arrives and sometimes, to our surprise, a student plagued by the proverbial "I-don't-care" attitude matures a little. The horizon where adulthood looms has a way of grabbing their attention and sobering their outlook. Reality slaps them upside the head and they realize time is running out and they have to become more responsible.

Teaching General Studies classes these past few years has taught me to be more forward looking when it comes to lost fifteen and sixteen-year-olds. Why? Because many who seemed unreachable their freshman and sophomore years begin to respond by the time they are juniors and seniors. It doesn't take much; sometimes just a summer's worth of maturity. With age kids begin to sort out the confusion of their childhood. They start adapting to some of the hard realities that rocked their world in younger years. They begin learning to accept things they can't change, like their divorced parents, and the failures of the dysfunctional adults in their lives.

Kids do grow up…**eventually**!

Sometimes they enter our rooms with a truck load of baggage and a trailer full of problems. We look at them, shake our heads and wonder, "Is it even possible to help them academically?"

We see their empty desk and mark them absent…again, but we continue to care. When they return to school we carefully gather their missing work and try to bring them up to speed.

Unfortunately, no matter how much we care, or how hard we work, we keep noticing their chair is empty, and when they are present, their head is down…usually along with their pencil. With a sigh of resignation we conclude: this student is not reachable, at least not right now.

Is it okay to feel that way?

Is it okay to concede?

Do we have permission to give up?

Should we feel bad if we can't give them what they need?

If you have read this far in *Roots of Apathy,* you are most likely one of those incredible educators who care deeply about the wounded and struggling children in our schools. You recognize that you are much more than a teacher or a counselor…you are a caregiver for those most needy walking around our campuses. Caregivers don't believe in throwaways, but the harsh reality is, we can't be a father or mother to every student who isn't properly nurtured at home. Sometimes teenagers move themselves beyond the reach of our help and outside the sphere of our influence. Sometimes all we can do is keep watching the horizon, hoping that something just around the corner might turn them in a new direction.

They could have a brush with some kind of disaster. They could face some sobering consequence for their irresponsible actions. They could even have an "epiphany moment" as a result of an unexpected encounter with someone who cares deeply about them… someone like you or me. Today they might be a total mess, but tomorrow? Who can say? We just never know when they might be ready, so we wait, and remain watchful.

We prod and encourage.

We speak the truth.

We talk straight.

When their behavior is unacceptable, our love is tough.

We set clear boundaries, and we don't coddle and enable. Despite their dysfunction, we always keep communicating that we see greatness in them. We remain hopeful that one day they might start believing that we got it right…that they <u>can</u> do better.

I've heard colleagues speak of these difficult students with frustration:

"They won't succeed."

"They're lazy and apathetic."

"They never do their work."

"They don't care about school."

"We're not going to be able to help them."

"Oh, I had them last year and they won't try."

"You're wasting your time."

Don't get me wrong, I'm not judging. I've felt the same emotions too, but more and more these days my response to that kind of murmuring has become…**"Not yet!"**

All those sentiments felt about a difficult student might be spot on at the present, but tomorrow, or next week, or next month, that kid might turn the corner…just **not yet**. I agree, some teens seem unreachable…at least **not yet,** and some don't want to change their behavior or even see the need to…well, **not yet**! Many young people are not mature enough…**yet**, to handle their personal problems and be successful in school at the same time…**not yet**!

With the really challenging students I find it helpful to adopt a **"Not Yet Policy."** It acknowledges that bad behavior is <u>not</u> okay, but it never burns the bridge back home. It leaves the door open for tomorrow and never surrenders hope.

With a **"Not Yet Policy"** in place I'm encouraged to simply do my very best, on this day, to reach the ones I can…those ready to change.

And the rest?

Maybe in time we can reach them, too…just "**not yet**".

Chapter Thirteen

Straight From the Heart

****

Students are going to write this chapter. The stories are theirs, straight from the heart and poured out on paper. There was no technical writing process used with this assignment, no rough draft, editing and final copy for most of them. For most of these "authors," the stories were too personal to have someone read. This was not a case of, "Hey Dad, Mom, could one of you read over my assignment before I turn it in?" The only changes from the original writing were a few grammatical edits and the removal of all identifying information; names of towns, schools and people. These writers could be from anywhere in America, or they could be sitting in your classroom right now. This may not be a chapter you read all in one setting. But it might be a good place to come one those days when teaching is hard and you need a fresh reminder that apathy has roots.

1. **"Where's My Daddy?"**

When I was in elementary school I got really good grades, but I was always an outcast. It didn't ever bother me until I was older though. Also, not knowing my dad has always affected me in a big way; not having someone to play baseball with, or tease and joke around with. So I never was completely happy growing up. I remember hearing kids talk about how much fun and cool their dad was and I just sat there, trying to understand why mine wasn't even around. I know my story isn't all that bad compared to others, but I can't imagine myself anywhere worse. I remember making up a dad, just so when people talked about theirs, I could talk about mine too.

2. **Replacing an Absent Father**

Ever since I was little I've had drama in my life. In first and second grade my mom and dad were together, but there was constant fighting. All the time all I would hear was fighting, and it got worse and worse. In third grade I remember I fell asleep on the couch one time and when I woke up my dad was dragging my mom down the hall by her hair into the kitchen. And then he broke a plate and threw it at her. She ended up having to get stitches. That night my mom called the cops and I watched my dad get arrested. After that my dad moved out and I never saw him for several years. Up until 5th grade I had good grades, but me and my mom were enemies. She always went out and brought guys to the house, but that never really got far, because every time I saw them I'd scare them away. I used to wait on the stairs for my mom to get home. The guys she brought home didn't usually stay very long because as soon as they walked in I would ask, "Who's this?" and tell them they were ugly I would scream and tell them to leave. I would call my mom names and have a total freak out, and they would leave. I did that for a long time and, as a result, my mom and I didn't talk much. In the sixth grade I stopped doing that, and my mom started seeing my step dad I have now. At first I liked him, but then I went back to my old ways and tried to scare him off. Well, instead of just leaving, he popped me in the mouth and made my nose bleed. After that I went crazy. I left my house for three days, but eventually got over it and came back. In the sixth grade I started hanging out with the wrong crew. I hung out in the "popular" group and thought I was cool. I started ditching, smoking weed and drinking.

In the seventh grade my dad tried to come back into my life. It was weird. He already had another wife and kids. One thing that really hurt me was that me and my dad had a special song that was "our" song ever since I was a baby (I was a daddy's girl back then) and I found out it had become his and his other step-daughter's song. That made me really angry and I felt replaced. Throughout seventh grade the same stuff went on. I smoked weed, drank and partied with my older cousin. I started going to my dad's every other weekend, because they went to court, but every time it was my dad's weekend I would leave and go to my friend's house.

In eighth grade my cousin became a model, so I started going to big parties in Vegas and LA; doing the same things; drinking and smoking. Freshman year I started ditching way more.

159

I still drank, smoked and I started going out and not coming home at night. I would come home wasted or high and I always got in trouble, but I didn't care. I still did it anyway. By the end of freshman year I wanted to stop coming to school. I was already so far behind that the whole last two weeks I didn't come at all.. Summer came, and I was never home. I went to parties a lot and drank. I got asked multiple times if I wanted to try coke, meth and all that, but I turned them down because of a bad past experience. Last year I tried meth one time when I was really high and I hated it. I promised myself to never try it again. In a way I'm kind of proud of myself. While they were all doing coke and crap, I was just thinking "that's nasty."

Recently I got caught with weed by my mom and I got in trouble, for once. They drug tested me to see what was in my system, it was just weed, but I got grounded; phone taken away and everything. I realized, it's stupid to try and be so messed up, so before school started I told myself, "I gotta do good this year." I haven't smoked weed since I got in trouble, or partied, and I'm not going to. Instead I spend the weekends with my boyfriend. That's my story.

3. <u>Absent Parents and the Party Life</u>

I think it's good for us to write about our life story. I have never thought about writing about my life. From first through seventh grade I never got lower than a C on a report card. In the seventh grade is when I first smoked week. I was playing football then and it really didn't effect my life. I started messing up in school when I became friends with this guy. Once I got into the drug life I became friends with a lot of new people. Doing drugs led me to start selling them. By freshman year I was getting high about every day. I was still playing football and my grades were still good, but by sophomore year something happened...I dropped out of football. That's when my grades dropped. I thought hanging out with my friends and smoking bud was more important that anything in my life. My junior year it was the same. I didn't play football and I was smoking more than ever, at least 4-5 times a day. All the money that I had went into bud. I really don't have a close relationship with my parents. They work a lot, and when they are not at work, they're out of town. My parents think its ok just to give me money to make up for the time they don't spend with me. So now it's my senior year and I'm in the same habit doing the same thing every day. Once you're in the party life it's hard to get out.

4. Sexual Abuse / Shame

I never really thought I would write my story, and to be honest, my mom doesn't want me to. She told me to lie about it. I don't really mind telling it though. This assignment is kind of weird to me and I never thought a teacher would ask this.

In kindergarten I lived with my grandma and visited my mom on the weekends. My mom is bipolar and gay. She lived in a backhouse at the time and the landlord had a nephew that was around 18 or so. When I went over to my mom's he would **rape** me every chance he got. I never said anything about it, because even *then I felt like it wasn't right, and was **ashamed** of it. I was first diagnosed with **ADHD** in kindergarten. When I was put on medication for it I started to get really good grades.*

*I was an "A" student during first and second grade, but I still had trouble concentrating in class. I was still living with my grandma and still being **sexually abused** on the weekends. My mom started seeing some lady that she worked with. She seemed nice and all, so it didn't bother me much.*

*My mom **moved** to be with her girlfriend in the beginning of my third grade year, but she let me stay behind with my grandma, so I could finish the third grade. Since she moved away, I didn't have to go to the backhouse, therefore the raping stopped, but I still never told anyone. About halfway through the year she came to visit and decided to **move** me to be with her. My grades dropped slightly, but I got them back up. The new town was about fifteen minutes from Mexico, so I was about the only white person there. This didn't bother me so much, at least not yet.*

*All the schools there were uniform schools and I wasn't used to it. My grades stayed up and I was mainly good in reading. I started noticing that the **other students were making fun of me** for being white. This is when it started to bother me.*

I was the highest A.R. reader in the school and I won a bike for it. I read 12th grade books and my grades where good. My teacher did algebra with us and I was good at it too. She pushed us all to be our best. The making fun of me was getting worse though, so I started getting **low self-esteem**. My mom and her girlfriend were always **fighting at home**, so I was crying a lot then.

In sixth grade the **bullying** got a lot worse; to the point of me hating myself and getting depressed. I had forgotten about what had happened to me kindergarten through part of third grade, but now I slowly started to remember and it only made the **depression** worse. My grades started bombing big time. I almost had **straight F's** that year. My mom and her now wife broke up so we had to **move** out.

We moved back to our old town and lived in a house my mom's friend rented out to us. My grade weren't getting any better either. At the end of the year we **had to move** out because, even though we paid our rent, the owners didn't pay for the house. That's when we moved in with my aunt in another town. At the time, she was going through a divorce of her own, so there was a lot of drama going on. Eventually she lost the house in the divorce, so we **moved** and my mom and her ex-wife tried to work things out again in the town by Mexico, but it didn't work. I didn't really have friends at this time. Instead I had people that hated me. My **self-esteem** was dragged down even more. Then we **moved again** back with my grandma. We stayed up there for about two weeks. Then we **moved** to Las Vegas with my aunt and her new husband. I moved there during finals. So it was kind of hard. Plus they do things really different there. They switched classes around almost every day. It was around then that I started **cutting myself**. My grades dropped back down because the classes were different from here. Over the summer we **moved** back.

*In freshman year I was cutting myself a lot. I **kept**
remembering when I was little. My younger cousin saw that what I
was doing and told my aunt, and she told my mom. **I finally told her**
that I was raped. When I told her a lot changed. I started going to
therapy and I soon became the black sheep of the family. I was kind
of out casted by them all. They didn't really want me around.
Especially when I started **sexting**. They all talked bad about me. I
know it was stupid of me to do.*

*To make things worse, about that time, my **grandpa died** in
front of me in the living room. I was **depressed** for a quite a while
after that.*

*Eventually, I ended up at this high school and my grades
started to improve. The teachers here make a good effort to help me;
like how you pushed me at the end of the year. My home life wasn't
good at all, though. There was way too much drama going on at
home. My mom and I were soon pushed away from the family. We
don't really talk to them much anymore. They say I'm a failure and
won't amount to anything. They say I look like a street walker,
because my hair and clothing are bright.*

*Now I am trying to pull myself together. I now have some
new motivation. I want to prove my family wrong; success is the best
revenge. I know that isn't a very good reason, but I'm tired of being
told I'm nothing, so I plan to turn everything around this year.*

5. A Father's Rejection: Bitterness, Anger and Depression

Ever since I can remember, I wasn't a great student; school just wasn't my strong suit. My worst subject was math. Right from the start it just never clicked in my brain. I remember seeing my old report card from my first school years and they all said the same thing, that I had a real problem in math. I chuckled a bit when I saw this. I thought, "Wow, I was bad at math since the beginning." But hey, who doesn't have a problem with math? In the second grade I moved to a new town, new people and a new school. I was very shy, so it took me a while to make one friend.

Since a young age I always felt I wasn't good enough, and that I was never going to accomplish anything in life. This is mostly because my father constantly reminded me of it. Now, a young boy hearing this from his father all the time can really see his self-esteem take a big hit, and that's exactly what happened to me. I was living in constant fear that if I didn't bring my homework home, or I didn't do it perfectly, that my father would scream at me. My mom even acknowledged that his words hurt more than his actions. At times I feel that he doesn't love me and just wishes that I was out of the house. He has repeatedly told me that he wants me out because he isn't going to raise a lazy, good for nothing son. I don't talk to my dad anymore. As soon as he comes home from work I go in my room in fear of being constantly criticized by him. If I had to pick one issue that holds me back in school I believe I would say depression. I have looked up depression on the internet and I have all the symptoms, although I didn't tell my mom or the school psychologist. I also have really low self-esteem, but thanks to the help of the mock trial team, and my friends, it has gotten better. But as soon as I get home and my father begins criticizing me, my self-esteem crashes back down, so I go into my room and just stay there for the rest of day. My mom says my dad is getting nicer towards us, but I don't see it. I still see him as the cold-hearted man I have always known. That's the main reason my grandma and aunts don't come to visit us. They say they just hated when he starts screaming. Of course my dad doesn't know this is the reason they don't stay the night, so he just blames my mom. This infuriates me!

My freshmen and sophomore years I did horrible in school. I had nearly all F's, and I'm behind 30 credits. Although I've been doing a lot better this year and I will continue to do better, I still had four F's, one D and a C on the last report card, but I'm going to do better this year.

I feel I'm headed on the right path this year. I'm more organized and I'm turning in my work. My goal for this year is to get a 3.0 for the first time in my life. It's not going to be easy, but it's a challenge I am now willing to accept.

My goals are to work more on my organization and to turn in my homework instead of just holding on to it, and letting it clutter up in my backpack. The things I'm going to do differently are I'm going to ask teachers for help, no matter how stupid the question might seem. I'm also going to stop being so lazy and putting everything off until the day its due. I'm going to change this year Mr. Hicks, and hopefully for the better.

6. <u>Adopted.</u>

I haven't always struggled in school. In third grade I had A's and B's, but then as time went on my grades fell, and so did I. I found out things I didn't want to believe.

The first thing that led to my downfall in school was that I found out the person I called dad wasn't really my dad. It turns out my dad left before I was born. I've never met him, and I don't want to.

In fourth grade my grades fell. Fifth and sixth grades were the same. Learning I was adopted led to fail every class. Then junior high came around and I started to party, drink and smoke. Things all went downhill from there. That's when I started getting into trouble with the cops because of fighting. That's all I did was fight. I didn't care and I gave up on myself.

Then I started high school where I kept doing the same things and I messed up and fell behind. But at the end of my freshman year I found this girl and she didn't know about my past. I started to tell her my story and she told me the only way her and I could be together is if I quit smoking, drinking, partying, fighting and getting into trouble, so that's what I did. I haven't been in trouble for over six months.

She saved me!

Without her I have no clue where I would be right now. On the 14th I will be clean and alcohol free for seven months. I love her for saving me. She tutors me every day and helps me with school. I truly am blessed.

Right now I am just trying to walk across that stage with my class, but then I'm hoping to go to college somewhere. My goals are to finish school, start a family and keep my head on straight. I'm ready to change. I have already started. I'm starting new and forgetting the past.

7. <u>Abused, Parents in Jail, Adopted</u>

Well, it all started when I was like three and my birth parents would always fight and do drugs around me, my brothers and my sisters. So when I was four I was adopted, but before that my birth parents were always running from the cops and we would have to move a lot.

My little brother doesn't know we are adopted so we can't really talk about it at all. My birth parents used to beat and abuse us all the time and make us starve. One time my birth mom broke my little sister's arm; she was four. My issues, or roots, are abuse, messed up parents and fear that they might find us and take us away from our adopted parents, but that probably won't happen because they are locked up in jail for a very long time. I am angry at my birth parents for doing all this to us. I think it's a lot better this year because I got baptized and gave my whole life to Christ. I feel like I'm loved and that I can learn better than before. I just had to forgive and forget my birth parents.

8. Alcoholism and Abuse

My life started really going bad when I was seven years old. I have a sister older than me and she had it even worse and I did. My parents were together since they were in their twenties, but my dad is an alcoholic and my parents were going through a lot when I was seven. My dad would hit us and do anything you can imagine when he was drunk. I never saw my mom happy when she was with him.

Finally me parents split up, so me, my sister and my mom moved in with my grandparents. Because of this I had to go to a different school, but my dad still didn't leave my mom alone, so we moved again to my mom's best friend's house. Of course this meant we had to move again, so we had to go to yet another school. My mom knew I was going through a lot and because of all the school changes, I didn't really learn things like I should have, so she decided to hold me back a year.

9. Stress at Home / Falling Behind at School

I think this assignment will help me figure out what needs to be changed and where I need to change my life style. I've never thought about writing my story before.

In kindergarten I was like every other kid. In first and second grade it was the same. In 3rd grade my grades started to slip because of my step dad. He would drink and get drunk, and then yell at us and come at me like he was going to hit me, but my mom wouldn't let him. They would split up...then get back together. I was always stressed because of this. I would get lazy with my school work, but somehow I would pass. I wouldn't put effort in school, but instead focused on having fun. I was stressed because I felt like I couldn't do anything right.

Right now, in school, I'm trying my hardest to keep my grades up. I'm not sure what my G.P.A. is, but I think my grades are pretty good. I believe I have no D's or F's.
I'm headed, I hope, to better days in school.. I'm ready to change. I've needed to change, but I haven't wanted to before. I will do anything to get those good grades.

10. Divorce / No One to Talk To

My story starts when I was only nine years old. I was spending the night at my friend's house having the time of my life. The next morning when I went home there was a huge truck parked in front of my house with all our stuff inside it. We were moving! My parents were getting a divorce, and at that time, I didn't understand why. My dad, three brothers and I left everything I ever loved...ever knew, in a heartbeat. Since then things haven't really been easy. I used to be able to tell my mom everything I was feeling, everything I was going through, but everything changed in my life.

Sophomore year I kind of just gave up. The whole year I didn't really care about school. I was just trying to get by. I didn't really do anything rebellious, but what I was doing wasn't really me, and I knew it. I kind of felt like I was alone and there wasn't really anyone I could talk to. My home life was great and I visited my mom almost every day, but I was never able to tell anyone how I felt. I had issues, but they didn't matter to anyone, so I had to just keep them inside most of the time. I've recently been going to church a lot more. I know the things I'm doing now won't be able to change my parents, and as for me, I'm the only person that can change my life. I'm just so tired of being tired.

Lately I've done all my school work. I actually study now and I'm learning to tell people how I feel instead of keeping it all inside.

11. <u>Divorce / Unhealthy Friends / Failing in School</u>

Elementary school started off good. I attended class every day and maintained good grades. School was easy for me at that point in my life. Little did I know it was about to go downhill.

Around third grade my parents divorced. I remember having to call the police on my parents multiple times for fighting. After that it was pretty much a blur. I began using drugs in Junior High and started failing in school. Finally my dad began pushing me to pass and I graduated.

High school started off great. I was passing my classes and had tons of friends. Unfortunately, I fell into the wrong crowd and started using prescription pills and alcohol. That's when I began failing in school again. Although I've dug myself into a deep hole I have chosen to change for the best. I currently moved in with my dad and started attending church. I have been sober for a little over a month now and I plan on completing high school the best I can.

12. <u>Homeless / Confused / Looking for Answers</u>

When I was in Junior High my mom started doing meth again, but this time it was because of her new husband. It wasn't long before they started fighting a lot and my step dad would break things, hurt people and get drunk. Somehow he always twisted things so it was me or my mom's fault. As time went on they started getting into drugs worse and worse. By this point my grades dropped from B's to D's.

To make things worse we never had much food in the house. We would have rice and potatoes, but that's about it. Then one day I went out and got the mail...and I noticed that my mom's truck was gone. There was a letter there for my mom and I held it up to the light and I read "Notice of Eviction." I started to cry because we lived far away from any family and there was no one there for us. We were going to be homeless if things kept going the way they were.

I remember this feeling...like I had to feel better, or I won't want to be here anymore. So I went on a search, a search for life beyond what I knew, and that's when I found marijuana. I did some research before I tried it and I found out that it wasn't a drug, and that it just multiplies your emotions and helps you pull your life together, and that's just what it did.

So I gave my mom the letter and she started crying and saying she was sorry. We packed up what we had and moved to another state and I was homeless up until about 3 to 4 months ago. Now my parents are in jail and I'm living with my grandma and going to school every day. So weed saved my family from going down the wrong road.

13. <u>Custody Battle / Truancy</u>

I lived with my dad when I was 4 until I turned 11. My dad took care of me while my mom was in jail. When she got out she tried to get me back, but my dad didn't want to give me up. She ended up taking my dad to court and got me back with shared custody.

When I went to live with my mom I was just starting 6th grade. We moved at the start of Junior High and I started at a new school. I was scared because it was a new place and I didn't know anyone. But even though I didn't know people I still managed to get good grades and stay out of trouble.

Then we had to move again in the middle of my 7th grade year. We moved back to our old town and I had another new school to go to, and new friends to make. I was terrified because I didn't know how these people would treat me. Before high school I moved out of my moms and into my nana's. Things got rocky and I had to move back in with my mom because my nana wanted me to have a better relationship with her, (my mom).

Over the summer my mom and I started arguing again. We never got along very well. That's when her boyfriend started getting into our fights and making them worse. My mom and him likes to fight a lot too and it doesn't help that my mom likes to drink.

10th grade came along and I just gave up. I was just so tired of it all. I was depressed and had anxiety when I was around a lot of people. I still do. About that time I started ditching school, my grades were in the drain and I was on my 4th truancy step so the school called my mom and set up a meeting. I finally decided to go see my counselor and tell her about everything to see if she could help me. She met with us all when I had to talk about my truancy step. When we were in there my mom would pass the blame onto anyone but herself. After the meeting I went to see my counselor again to see what she thought. She told me my mom was going to be a hard nut to crack. She just doesn't listen. The guy from the office that we met with came in. He asked if my mom drank, and I said yes. He then told me that he could smell it on her. Unfortunately, not a lot changed after that, instead, it got worse bit by bit. My mom's boyfriend wanted to know what happened in the meeting, and what I said to my counselor. When I didn't tell him he got mad and told me that I had to move over the summer. We never talked after that because he told me I was going to be worthless like my family. My mom didn't even argue with him about it.

It's summer time now and I'm in summer school because I messed up so bad. Just yesterday my mom kicked me out and I had to miss school because I had to find a place to live. I'm living with my Nana again and hoping that I can get through high school without getting in trouble. Perhaps even get good grades.

So I just have one thing left to say, "What's going to happen in my life now?"

14. Don't Want to Write My Story

The feelings I have on writing this story aren't horrible, but I'm definitely willing to write some of it out. I can't remember all of my past, in fact, it is very fragmented and not fully comprehensible to me. I have thought about writing my story, but not at my young age. It's something I thought about doing when I am older, like around 70 or 80.

The first years that I can recollect are around the age four or five; not sure exactly. My mom and my dad were having troubles with their relationship and my two older sisters and I kind of understood what was going on. The problems weren't physical between my parents, just not connecting like they used to I guess. My two sisters both have a different father than me, but I didn't care at all about that. They were the closet to me and I loved them. I also had two older brothers that weren't my mom's, but my dad's. They were still close to me too, but not as close as my sisters were to me. My brothers weren't with us all the time, but with their mom and living there own story.

So as my mom and my dad were splitting up, my sisters and I were staying with my grandparents and they also were having a little trouble of their own. My grandpa was in the Vietnam War and I cannot even fathom what horrors he saw there, but when he got back he was into drugs and doing heroin for a while; I guess to escape his own thoughts and for other personal reasons of his own. But he's been clean for a pretty long time now.

One time, when I was little, I wandered around the house and I found myself in his room. Being a curious little child, and getting into everything, I went through my grandparent's dresser and got into my grandpa's side of the dresser. I remember finding a syringe with a dark fluid in it with a blue tint and being young and careless, I started to play with. That was not a good idea because I ended up sticking myself with it. I went to my mom and told her and she looked at me with a crazed look on her face and started to scream at me. I blacked out after that and don't remember anything for years after that moment. That's my earliest memory. The next thing I remember is when I was in middle school. I'm living with my mom and two older sisters now because she and my dad split up. My mom remarried, so I have a step dad now and they have a son and a girl. My step dad and I did not get along at all and he was very mean to me and only me so that caused stress and problems, I don't know why he was mean to me but I think it was because something happened in his childhood that made him that way.

When in middle school, my grades started to drop and this was probably because I started to smoke weed in 7th grade. So my grades weren't what they could be and my mom found out that I was smoking weed and I was punished many times but I still did not stop no matter how much trouble I got into. Next was high school, and I'm still smoking and living with my mom and all. I also started to do some hallucinogens which really change my whole life and perception on things that I can't even explain. Things go bad and I get caught smoking before school because I smelled way too much.

Then after that my mom was tired of it all and called my dad and said I'm going to be living with him now. This was after I had already gotten in trouble many times for about the same reason about a dozen times over again. So my mom took me out of the school before they could expel me. My dad picked me and all my belongings up a couple days later and it was a little rough but I knew in my head that it was for the better. So now I'm living with my dad and his new wife, my step-mom who also is kind of a sour person towards me and doesn't really like me at all just like my step-dad, in Bakersfield and I'm in this new high school trying to make some friends and it's my senior year before I go off to college.

I have turned a new leaf and am not doing all the things that got me off my path to success. Living with my dad is way better because there's a lot less stress, but still not stress free. I am extremely close to my mom and I love her a lot and I have apologized to her for all the stress and heartbreak I put her though. My grandparents are still together and they both love each other very much. That's really my story, there's more but I just can't tell you, or anyone for that matter, the true detail of it all, but the rest of my life is for me to write.

15. <u>Feeling inferior / Depression</u>

I don't mind writing my life story. There isn't a whole lot to say, but it does help to write it down, if only to get it off my chest. I've considered telling my closest friends when they asked after I left last year, but I never felt ready to tell anyone.

Elementary school, for the most part, was great for me. I was one of the happiest kids in kindergarten through fifth grade. My teachers loved me. I was polite, bright, articulate, sweet...basically any word that describes a good kid in elementary school described me. My problems first appeared in sixth grade. Before sixth grade I was elite. I took great pride in everything I did. I was always confident. Nothing really changed that year except I lost my confidence. I was no longer elite. I went from being one of the best, to run of the mill. It wasn't some big dramatic thing, but just little things that changed. I didn't want the ball passed to me on the playground anymore, I stopped wanting to be the center of attention and I got my first B in school. Nobody noticed a difference, but me.

I've always wished I could go back and be that version of me again. I liked that guy a lot more. My inferiority complex grew progressively worse after that year. Junior High went by with pretty much no changes to my demeanor. I got A's and B's in school. I seemed happy enough, however, my confidence issues were growing worse every day. My academic downfall started my freshman year. I failed a couple classes and began feeling depressed and lost.

Sophomore year went great but junior year my life officially fell apart. I failed pretty much all of my classes and became so depressed I couldn't get out of bed. I spent most of my time crying. I left school at the beginning of the second semester and felt a lot better afterwards.

I'm doing well in school so far this year, but we're only two weeks into senior year. I have a 4.0 and got an A on the only test I've taken thus far. Now hopefully I'm headed off to college. I didn't do well enough in high school to go straight to a university but I'm going to a JC and try to graduate in two years, then go to on to a university. Then I want to get a job and live a happy successful rest of my life.

16. <u>Poverty</u>

I feel that this assignment is an opportunity for troubled kids to write their own stories, and for those who have been through tough times in their life to get it out of their system. I have been thinking about writing my own story because, to be honest, there's so much to talk about, and I think my story would be helpful to other people and encourage them not to lose hope when things change in life.

In first and second grade I didn't struggle that much in school. I got along with everyone and I was reading a lot. Life was good back then, even though I didn't have a dad around.

When third grade came I changed schools because it wasn't working out living in my brother's house. Because of mistakes that my mom and I have made, my brother's wife doesn't like us around. I think she hates us because she never talks to me…so it's awkward. My brother wanted me and my mom to move out so we moved into the ghetto. The place we were living didn't have any rooms. It was weird. It was my mom, my other siblings and I, but we made the best of it. I was hanging a lot with thugs and drug dealers while we lived there.

In the fourth grade I was popular at school. I had the best friends anyone can ask for and I was doing well in my class. My friends made living in this bad area bearable. My brother would pretend to care and would always check on us to make sure we were doing alright, but it was a bunch of bull crap. My mom and I had to walk 45 minutes to get to his house and to go shopping for food because we didn't have a phone or money to call him.

Fifth grade came and I was really sad in this house. How were we supposed to eat? We had nothing but beans. It pissed me off because my brother and the rest of the family were eating like royalty and we were eating like peasants. My mom cried and would get stressed out, but something kept us close. I guess you can call it hope. There would be times when we will run out of beans and corn was the only food to eat. My mom would be going around asking for money or going to a Mexican store and asking for food to feed her children. I was sad and scared seeing this happening to us. The only things that made me feel positive were my friends.

Then it got worse. We got our electricity shut off in the house for about eight months. It was scary because the stove ran off electricity. It tore me up inside because it was like the family didn't care about us anymore. Scary, crazy people were moving in and out. We lived in the ghetto, so that was kind of normal, but I kept on making new friends and I liked how they understood how I was living, especially the thugs and drug dealers.

By sixth grade I had had enough. I didn't care anymore. I wasn't hanging around the house that much and I just got tired of being poor with my faded clothes. So I started helping out the thugs selling drugs when they couldn't because the cops were watching them. They watched over me and protected me. When my brother came back to visit us he saw what I was doing, and saw who I was hanging out with, and he moved us somewhere else. Finally we had normal food and electricity.

17. <u>Divorce and Unhealthy Friends</u>

My parents have been divorced since I can remember. There's literally not a day I can remember when it was my dad, mom, brother and me. With my parents' divorce I've never been close to my dad. I see him when I have to, until recently. Since the divorce, my mom and dad both have gotten remarried and they both have had two kids each. Having to live with my mom and step dad isn't that bad, but being the oldest in the house, I have a lot more responsibility. I'll have to watch my little sisters, pick them up from school and get stuff for my parents sometimes.

Going to my dad's used to be kind of awkward, but cool, because I would never have to do chores. I wouldn't see my dad for about a month then I would have to go to his house. But my dad is the funniest person I know, and just a cool dad in general. I used to think he wasn't that good of a dad because he wouldn't pay child support, but he would give his two kids anything they wanted. It seemed like he would just talk bad about my mom all the time and like he didn't care about me or my brother.

When high school started I had to go to a different school then all my friends from junior high. Starting over with new friends wasn't that hard for me. Finding the right group for my life wasn't really a priority. I hung out with the kids that smoked all the time. My best friend would smoke weed all the time and she would ask if I wanted to, but I never would, because I didn't want to get in trouble.. But then one day I smoked with some friends, and I thought I was really cool. So from that day on I would smoke a lot. Anything else my friends would do I would do too. Eventually we all tried other drugs, but when I moved to schools I stopped all of that. At this new high school I started hanging out with athletes and they didn't party, so I didn't have to. I realize now that you can be influenced by the people you hang out with. The people I used to hang out with made me lazy and got me focused on fun, not school.

I'm behind credits now and I might not graduate. Things have to change...I have to change in order to graduate and have a better future. My life is going by so fast. I need to make it worth living and not be a failure in the end.

18. <u>No Father</u>

I really don't want to do this assignment. I've never had to tell someone my story before but I guess there's always a first.

It all started before I was born.

Well, my mom and dad were really never married. After my mom found out she was pregnant with me she also found out that my dad is crazy. My dad had to take medication; but he didn't take it.

He was an alcoholic, and he also did drugs. My dad got mad at my mom one day and went and destroyed her apartment while she was at work. He made holes in the walls, broke that bathroom mirror and made a mess.

I never really knew my dad. I think the last time I saw him I was five years old. I can still remember the day I learned he would be gone. My mom and I went to my grandpa's house (my dad live with his mom and dad still) because I wanted to show my dad my pet fish I got from Pet's Smart. When I knocked on the door my grandpa answered and he said that he needed to talk to my mom. I said, "Well, she's in the car waiting for me," so he went over and told her what had happened to my dad, and where he was at. After they were done talking I went back to the car and my mom told me my dad went on vacation but I didn't understand what she meant. I asked my mom why didn't my dad take me with him, and she told me because he couldn't. So as I got older I didn't know what to tell my friends about where my dad was, so I just said that I don't have a dad; that he went away somewhere. Not knowing my dad doesn't bother me at all; maybe when I was little, but not now. I really don't even know who my dad is. If he was to pass right by me in the store, I wouldn't know him. I stopped going around my dad's family after my grandpa died. I was around six years old.

Sometimes there's a part of me that feels like there's something missing, but I don't let it bother me. I have a great step dad, and he is my little brother's dad. He's like a dad in many ways, and sometimes I even call him dad.

19. <u>Video Games</u>

Ninth grade year was the start of my gaming career. Gaming could possibly be the worst choice I could have made. It really hurt my academics, but I didn't care. Gaming was my new life. I gamed from three o'clock in the afternoon to 2:30 a.m.; basically from the time I got home from school, to the time I went to sleep. I hardly even ate or slept. My morals dropped as well as my academics. Now my grades have dropped from C's to F's. All of that brought me to this stressful point I'm at today. I'm behind twenty credits, doing regular school and adult school both semesters. If I could go back and do everything differently my life might be a bit easier.

20. <u>Dyslexia</u>

Second grade was the hardest year of my life. I know what you're thinking, second grade? Why, that's supposed to be a time filled with monkey bar races, endless amounts of glitter, and of course, nap time. But alas, I was too preoccupied to enjoy those festivities. In this gloomy year, every student was required to take the dreaded eye examination. Those who did not pass this test were given the excruciating burden of...nerdiness. I was given this burden when I acquired my new, life-long accessories. As if glasses weren't a big enough encumbrance, I went to the orthodontists for the first time that year—and that malicious man gave me braces. Now if you thought braces hurt in high school, imagine me, the poster child for innocence, feeling the full extent of metal's hatred. In one year I had gone from the adorable kid with an over-sized head, to a four-eyed brace-face. Needless to say, there were quite a few crocodile tears that year.

Oh, it almost slipped my mind! And in second grade I was diagnosed with dyslexia. Dyslexia is probably the most perplexing and comical challenge that I have ever had. Having a learning disability, I was forever given the excuse to fail. All I had to say was, "Hey, I'm dyslexic," to any academic slip up that occurred and I could be content with mediocrity for the rest of my life. But my parents were never the kind of people who acknowledged excuses; my mother constantly reminded me that I was anything but average, and that settling for less, no matter the reason, wasn't good enough. I remember a time when teachers just hoped that I would be average: none really recognized I could be more. After many struggles in elementary school, and numerous remedial classes and tutors, I was moved into the general population, or as I liked to call it, "normal" classes. Dyslexia has proven to me that limitations only exist in our minds. When I was applying for the Gate and Honors program as a freshman, I was advised not to take that road because, with my history, college prep classes would better suit me. I am currently a senior who has taken eight Gate and Honors classes and I have passed them all. I think it is safe to say, my freshman advisor was mistaken.

Being Dyslexic, verbal slip ups occur often. I grew up saying things incorrectly. I would ask my dentist, "Can I go to the choy test now?" Or I would exclaim to my comrades, "I love cakecups!" After these blunders, a feeling of exasperation, as well as embarrassment, would follow. It has taken me quite some time, but I now am able to triumphantly laugh at myself. I currently view these bloopers as a little extra spice to my life. Dyslexia has taught me humor is medicinal: it can take the sting out of any awkward, dyslexic moment.

I am now standing at a threshold in my life. College is on my doorstep...waiting. Inside me is still the little four-eyed, brace-face second grader, afraid: afraid of what my peers might think, afraid of something new, and afraid that there may be obstacles I cannot overcome. I shall be attending college in the fall and I once again will be applying for the honors program. I have met all the requirements except for one, my SAT score. I have taken this, oh so confounding test, three times, and I shall take it three more until I prove that a dyslexic with straight teeth, horrible eye sight, and unclenching stubbornness is more than sufficient enough for any honors program.

The purpose of this is not to indulge in some convoluted ego that I may have, but instead, to share my experience. Inspiration is, in every human being, what we want, and what we hope to give to others. I might not be the person people aspire to be but since dyslexia has been proven to be a genetic disorder, the probability of my children having it will be high. So I will tell my children, as my mom told me, that they are anything but average and that settling for less, no matter the reason, is not good enough. And maybe, just maybe, these little four-eyed braces-faces of my own will look up at me and be inspired.

21. <u>Cutting / Eating Disorder / Panic Attacks</u>

I don't remember much from elementary school. I do remember that I had a few good friends at school and in my neighborhood, but other kids didn't like me. After that my dad moved out and my parents got a divorce. I didn't see him for quite a while. When I did see him we rarely spent time together.

I got my first C at the end of fifth grade and I realized that no one really cared, so all of middle school I didn't do anything. I didn't care about school at all. I was depressed and thought I wouldn't live past 8th grade, maybe not even 7th, so I thought "screw it." I barely showed up, never did homework and I didn't pay attention in class. 6th grade was when I started to let kids really get to me. I started hurting myself because of what other kids said. My mom was almost never home and I was always stuck watching my brother. 7th grade I moved schools and I had a big group of friends and people liked me. I was happier, but still was taking things out on myself. 7th grade was also the year that my dad got into a fatal car accident. Before that I didn't talk to him because I was furious at him. I wish that I had. 8th grade was alright. I had a really great friend. She helped me through almost everything. Kids were kind of mean to me, but she always stood up for me. I was a bit happier in 8th grade.

Ninth grade is when things got really bad. I started doing online school in October because I thought I would be happier and get better grades if I was away from everyone. I was for a while, but not for long. I fell into an eating disorder. I lost about 15 pounds within three weeks. I wanted to stop, but it's very difficult. I'm still struggling with it every day.

This year I'm back in public high school and I'm not really sure how I feel about it. I had an anxiety attack on the first day and I have been getting them at least once a day. It's gotten worse since I haven't been in a regular school for a while, and now that I am, my nervousness is overwhelming. I want to do good in school, but it's just hard for me.

22. Fear / Suicide

When I was younger my house never really felt like "home" to me. My older sister and I never felt comfortable at home, we were always scared. My dad has always been kind of a ruff man and he had always been verbally abusive to my mom. We all knew never to voice our opinion over his or he would get mad and act out. To everyone around us; church, family, neighbors and friends, we looked like a perfect family. Don't get me wrong; they loved me and my sister, but my dad had a hard time showing it. My mom grew up in a church home and she was one of those "Pastors daughters". Grandpa would do anything to keep a good reputation with the church.

When my mom was eight years old she was molested by one of her family's close friends who was sixteen, and my grandpa did nothing. His reputation was so important he didn't want a scratch on it. My mom starting struggling with depression when she was very young. She and my dad met in high school and then got married the day he turned eighteen. Ever since I was little all I could remember was fighting constantly. When I started first grade I met my first best friend. I would go to school every day and tell her the stories about my parents fighting. We both had that in common. My grades were overall very good. I loved school because that meant I didn't have to go home.

When I was about six years old my mom came and got my sister and I after school. We arrived home and I just remember her not letting us out of the car. We just sat in the garage with the car running. My mom didn't seem normal. She started crying and we kept asking if we could get out because we were scared. We found out a couple years later that it was her **first attempt to commit suicide**, with us in the car. Soon my little sister was born and I was a proud older sister, but after she was born the fighting got worse.

When I was about ten years old I was being more of a mom to my sister than I was a sister. My dad turned to alcohol and my mom barely looked at us. I would fake sick all the time in fifth and sixth grade when my dad was off work so I could make sure nothing bad happened between my mom and dad. When I was in the eighth grade my parents were at my little sisters' choir concert. It hadn't even been fifteen minutes before they were back home. My mom *came running in, grabbed something off the counter, and then my dad came in yelling at her. He asked me where she went and I replied, "She's in your room." Shortly after that I heard shouting and pounding. It sounded like someone had been thrown into a wall. I ran down the hallway thinking my dad had beat my mom. I yelled at him and shortly realized the bath room door had been broken down. As I looked into the bathroom; pills everywhere; a woman I thought I knew standing and looking blankly into my eyes; apologizing over and over. I didn't know her. It was like I was looking into black eyes; evil, this woman that had raised me.*

*I remember every detail of that night. My mom had **tried to kill herself the second time**. That night I found out who my mom really was. I questioned if she even loved us. If she hated my sisters and I so much that she didn't want to live, or be here with us anymore. I was confused and didn't know the meaning of it. I knew I had to hide it from my little sister, because she was so young and needed to feel loved. I tried my hardest to keep her happy. I noticed my mom acting more strange; like a teenager would usually act. Then my dad found out my mom had been talking to a twenty three year old across the world.*

The fights got so much worse then. My dad was furious and my mom got more depressed and started blaming us for everything. She thought good was bad, and bad was good. My dad brought up marriage counseling at one point. He wanted things to change for us, but my mom didn't. Our family was falling apart piece by piece. My dad started using horrible words in the fights calling my mom a slut, a whore; anything to break her down. They both were wrong, but us kids never had the nerve to stand up to him. My mom got in the car one day and left for five days without a word; nothing. School was starting up again and not knowing if my mom was dead scared us.

*The day before freshman year my mom came back and all hell broke loose. That's when I was at my lowest. I had been caught sneaking out multiple times and giving alcohol to my "friends". I started to party a lot with the people I thought were my friends. Two months into my freshman year, and close to Christmas, my parents had a huge fight. They had started marriage counseling a couple weeks before the fight. My sisters and I thought my mom was getting better; we were wrong. That night my parents were fighting and she reached for a gun in the safe on my dad's side of the bed. She had **tried suicide for the third time**. I could hear my dad telling her to set it down and to think about the kids. I remember sitting in the hallway praying with my little sister that it would all end.*

23. <u>Alternative High School</u>

My home life definitely wasn't the best environment for an elementary school student. My parents had divorced when I was four years old and my dad moved a lot. He was an alcoholic and momma loved meth more than her kids, so I wasn't home very much. I always had good grades, a 4.0 all the way until sixth grade. My elementary years were fun for me. I was a troublemaker in the neighborhood because I was never home. I wanted attention from my parents, negative or positive; either way didn't matter.

Sixth grade summer was when I started going downhill. It started with choosing the wrong group of friends in seventh grade. Instead of staying on top of school and focusing on getting good grades, I was focused on drugs, alcohol and getting laid. All of my friends were older than I was and I just went with the flow and got sucked into a life I loved at the time. I just didn't realize that the decisions I made in seventh grade would affect me throughout high school. My grades dropped dramatically in one year. I stopped playing football and almost got expelled for fighting and other bad behaviors. In eight grade I continued down this path and ended up getting expelled towards the end of the year. The whole time my parents were fighting for custody of me and my brother. My dad ended up winning us and I was happy, not because I liked him more, but because he had a lot more money than my mom and that meant getting more of whatever I wanted.

Freshman year I started going a little too hard with the partying and drinking and what not. My dad had money and he just threw it to me because I had passing grades and played sports; he thought everything was fine. Towards the end of freshman year the cocaine abuse got really bad to where I was doing bumps in the bathroom between classes. Finally I got expelled because I got in a fight in math class. After freshman year I got sent to Teen Challenge for 12-16 months, but I got kicked out for beating up a kid that was talking crap about my dad. After that I went to a different public high school for a little bit then dropped out altogether. Eventually I ended up in juvenile hall for two months. When I got out I went to an alternative school, but I got arrested again and that got me sent to a camp for boys for seven months. All total I have wasted 17 months of high school that I am now trying to make up.

The main distractions for me that make it hard to focus in school is just the lack of support I get from my parents. My parents have given up on me and are trying to make me do what they want, for the most part. My dad is so convinced that I'm going to fail all my classes and dropout that he signed a paper saying that he will pay me $1000 for each quarter I complete with a 2.0GPA. He also said he would buy me a brand new truck if I graduate, but it has to be a Ford.

24. <u>Depressed Parents / Drugs / Gambling</u>

I don't really remember much from elementary school. I do recall that I lived in an apartment and my sister and I would go to our babysitter's house after school until our mother got off work. In kindergarten I lived with my mom and her boyfriend and we were kind of in poverty. She was on drugs and such, and she did not look very well. A couple days after my birthday one year my mom decided that she didn't want us to get caught up in her trouble and everything she was into, so she had our grandma come and pick us up and we moved to a different town.

For a couple years we lived with our grandmother and life got better. I was a good student in that school, I got A's and B's, and did all of my homework. One day my grandfather got tired of me and my siblings and threatened to put us in foster care. A couple weeks later my dad came to California and took us away to another state. My sister and I were excited, but kind of sad, because we were leaving our family.

So we moved there in January. I was in the second grade when we moved and for several years I got great grades. Toward the end of fifth grade my nana (my dad's mom) passed away and it really hit my dad hard. He went into a depression for about a month. A few years went by and then my grandpa died too. My dad was still recovering from his mom's death and now his dad died. He went into a huge depression and was angry and hateful to everyone. He barely ever came home at night so I had little hope in school, and little, or no supervision. That's when I started staying out late at night and basically doing whatever I wanted. I wasn't home a lot and my dad got back into drugs and back into the Casino life. Pretty much every night he was with his girlfriend at the casino, or doing drugs. He rarely was home to see me and eventually he quit working. What little money he made he wasted at the Casino and usually, when he came home, he had no money at all. Because of this he couldn't pay the bills, so we ran out of electricity all the time. He even stopped making the car payment, so he would hide the car in the back yard in case they tried to repo it. He also stopped going to church and such, so he had no backbone to keep himself happy.

I came home one time after school and when I got off the bus and went to my room I noticed that some of my stuff was gone. I

194

looked all over the house and couldn't find it, so I texted my brother and it turned out my dad sold my stuff to pay for drugs and the Casino. I was so angry I didn't even go to school for the next two days. I had had it with my dad, so I called my grandma and mom and told them what happened. They said if I wanted to move back to California I could, so I took them up on their offer and got me a ticket for right after 8th grade graduation.

The next school year I started as a freshman at a good high school with new friends. I decided it was time to change. Although I didn't change all at once I passed both freshmen and sophomore years. Now I'm a junior and life is going great. I had a rough past, but I'm going to a good school, I have good grades again and I'm looking toward the future.

25. <u>Overdose in Class</u>

I was never really a good student. For some reason it was cool to fail and not try in school and that's how I was. I didn't really get in much trouble at school, but I had started smoking pot and trying new things by seventh grade. I started because my brother had gotten into that stuff and I was doing everything he was doing at the time. My parents never knew anything was going on until I was in the eighth grade. That's when I started getting caught being high and drunk.

The choices I made in high school really changed me. When I was a freshman I pretty much didn't care about anything, including myself, and I pretty much did anything I could, so I was never sober.

My friends and I had nothing going for us and everyday was just wasted on getting messed up. I was smoking weed every day and doing stupid things with my friends, like ecstasy on the weekends, not caring how bad it was for me. I made the mistake of getting myself into pain killers and I used them daily, taking stupid amounts before school in the morning. I didn't know what addiction was, or that it could ever happen to me. I never thought much about all the dumb stuff that I was doing and then one day I ended up overdosing in my English class. Right there in front of everyone I had a seizure. I could write about that experience for days because, as weird as it sounds, I learned so much from that situation. It sounds crazy, but it kind of made me feel more experienced and smarter than most kids today, kind of because I already went down that road when I was young and I know what not to do now.

26. <u>Dad Killed / Fear of Failure</u>

When I was in the sixth grade I got the news that my dad had been in a car accident and had passed away. I know for a fact that this changed me so much, but I don't even know how to explain it. My grades dropped in my classes, but I wasn't doing it on purpose. I know now it had to do with his death.

Once I got to junior high I was just mad about everything. I didn't care much about anything at all. At my school everybody knew people who used drugs and drank, and my friends were not the best influence on me. I had become a bad student who didn't listen in class and who didn't do his work. By the time eighth grade rolled around I started getting into trouble.

Once I got suspended for ditching school to go smoke with a friend. I got in so much trouble that year that I ended up not graduating from the eighth grade. High school didn't start out much better.

My freshman and sophomore years didn't go very well and I got behind in credits and ended up in a General Studies class to try and get back on track. I have some pretty good friends now who are helping and encouraging me. I feel like I have gotten a lot wiser than I used to be and I know what has to be done. The biggest distraction for me now is this fear that I have, fear of not passing. I get this feeling that I am too dumb and I'm scared I won't graduate.

27. <u>Restraining Order / Custody Battle</u>

Ever since I was little I always had good grades. Sometimes I would even get on the honor roll. When I was about ten years old my mom and dad started having problems and they would fight a lot and argue about anything. My dad was, and still is, very controlling. If he didn't get his way he would get mad. Sometimes he would refuse to talk to anyone until you would say that he was right and beg him to talk to you. There were times my dad would ignore my mom for weeks. I had a feeling they were not going to stay together, and that my dad would eventually leave.

When I was eleven that feeling came true and my parents got a divorce. My mom even filed a restraining order against my dad, because he would follow her, and basically stalk us. One time I was sitting on my bed when I decided to go get a snack from the kitchen. I noticed a knock on the back door and it was my dad. He told me to open the door, so I did. Being little, I didn't know any better. When he got in the house he went straight to my mom and started telling her to get up and go with him. She told him no, but he didn't care. He grabbed her and they took off in the car. I didn't see my mom until around midnight. She came home and my dad got arrested that night for hitting my mom. She had finger prints on her arm and bruises. Even till this day I think it's my fault that my mom got hit because I opened the door.

Eventually court day came and my brother and I had to choose who we wanted to live with. My brother chose my dad, and I chose my mom. Every time I went to my dad's house he would try to brainwash me into thinking my mom was a bad person and that he was the victim. He would argue with me because I would defend my mom and sometimes I would get so mad I would call her and ask her to come pick me up. When she would come my dad would start arguing with her and one time, when I was twelve, I yelled at him and told him I didn't want to come visit him anymore.

We still argue to this day, especially when he says something bad about my mom. I've heard him tell me I was a lying, spoiled brat; that I was stupid because I wouldn't tell him something he wanted to know. When it comes to being spoiled, I know I'm not. My mom didn't have a lot of money because my dad didn't pay child support. I've seen her cry because she couldn't pay the bills or give me things that I needed.

All these stresses affected me in high school. I had two bad years because I just stopped caring, but now I'm trying to get back on track with my school. I want to make my mom proud. In spite of all the mental abuse from my dad, my life is ok, I guess. Things are actually getting better. My dad is cooling down with all the arguing when I go over to his place and my mom is trying her hardest to make my life great. Now all I have to do is graduate and start my life.

28. <u>Poverty / Money Spent on Alcohol</u>

My home life was pretty regular until about third grade. That's when my mother began drinking heavily. Her and my dad occasionally drank before that, but for my mom, it turned into binge drinking. Whenever she drank she would become incoherent, belligerent and violent towards anyone in the house for no reason. Eventually she would start fights with my dad. The more they fought the worse it got. At one point my mom hit my dad in the mouth. When she realized what she had done she called the police on herself. After being locked up for a few days my mom came back home. My dad started getting ulcers during this time from all the stress. Soon after my mom's drinking problems my grades began to drop. I was too distraught about what was happening at home and lost my focus at school.

During this time my dad's friend moved into the house because he didn't have a house anymore. That really upset things. When my dad went to work my mom would get so intoxicated she would cheat on my dad with his best friend. Everything home-wise went downhill from there. The house got dirty because no one would pick up their trash and laundry and my dad's friend started doing marijuana in the garage. Periodically the electricity would get turned off because the bill money got spent on mom's alcohol and for my dad's best friend. Finally, after six months, my dad caught them cheating, so my dad moved out of our house and into my grandmother's house. By sixth grade my parents were divorced.

In middle school my grades continued to be pretty low. I lingered on my mom and dad's divorce more than I should have and my schooling suffered. My dad would always ground me for having terrible grades and not doing my work. I deserved it, but nothing improved very much.

In time my parents each moved into very different houses. My dad moved into a three bedroom, two bathroom upper/middle class house and my mom moved into a two bedroom, one bath apartment in a bad part of town. My sister and I had to trade off, staying with mom for a week, then dad for a week. At my mom's apartment she shared a queen-size bed with her boyfriend, my dad's old best friend, while my sister and I shared a room with a twin bed. The electricity would periodically get turned off because the childcare money my mom would get from my dad would get spent on alcohol, a new TV or cell phones instead of something we needed, like clothes, food or water bottles.

After a month or two my mom got extremely drunk one night and came to my sister and me on the war path. She came into the kitchen, picked us up by our hair and carried us to our rooms. She dropped us on our beds and yelled at us to go to bed, even though it was only 7pm. We were both too scared to leave our room, so we stayed and cried ourselves to sleep. At school the next day I called my grandparents and told them everything. The police got involved and my dad got full custody of my sister and me. We are both happy that we got out of that horrible place.

29. Broken Trust

When I was young my parents decided to get a divorce. The man I call my father had a short fuse and was very abusive. The alcohol in his system justified his excuses in his own mind, but his hands beat my mother one too many times. After ten years, she finally built up enough courage to leave that pathetic excuse for a husband. During this time, school wasn't a problem for me. From what I can remember, home life didn't affect my school work and my ability to learn. Teachers liked me and I received good grades.

After my parents went to court, my mother got custody of my siblings and I and my so called dad got us every other weekend. Everything was going smoothly and the separation wasn't hard on me, even though I was a daddy's girl when I was small. Once he started to drink the anger and rage took over his life, and *unfortunately, my family's life as well. He spit in my brother's face when he asked for a bath and phones were thrown at me if I wanted to call my mom. The words he would scream rang in my ears as my little sister wept on the couch, not knowing what to do. My "wonderful" father broke promises he should have kept. He got our hopes up, only to shoot them down, and he corrupted our fragile minds before we even knew what hit us.*

At school my life was still very bright and nothing bothered me at all. I was just a kid being carefree. Away from school, however, the abuse from my dad was becoming unbearable. He was mentally, physically and emotionally breaking me down. My mom saw what was happening and she went back to court and got us out of that situation. After that, and up to now, my father can only see us if he pays someone to watch him with us on visitation days. So far he hasn't made that effort, not even once.

I'm in high school now, and looking back I understand my situation better. My father was an alcoholic who lashed out at his family. He screwed up my trust, so now I have trust issues, mostly with the male gender. Freshman and sophomore years I drank and smoked weed to numb my pain (which I thought I didn't have). I tried so many times to rekindle a relationship with my father, but there is no chance. My father, who the family refers to as a "sperm donor", is a beer-belly, broke man, with no wife or kids. He won't change, so I have moved on. My goal now is to make something of my life. That is my story!

30. Pot / Spice / Crystal Meth…Rehab

I was so excited when I finally reached middle school. All my homies were there with me, but none of them did drugs or alcohol. They were good kids, but I was a little trouble maker. I ditched classes, cussed at my teachers and got in a lot of fights. All this trouble got me moved to a different school, and that was the worst thing that ever happened to me. I met some new people and started hanging out with the wrong crowd. During the summer before eighth grade I started smoking pot. I tried a little at first, but then I started doing it a lot. By the time eighth grade began I was already known as a "pot-head". Eighth grade was the year that changed me. I was smoking pot every single day. There was never a day that I didn't smoke.

One day the homies said they wanted to buy some spice. When I heard that I just thought spice was a new type of weed, so I started hitting it, but then I noticed the taste and I knew right away that it wasn't weed. I liked it though. The high was amazing, but it didn't last long at all.

Freshman year came along and I started drinking and smoking. My third day of school I got expelled for drawing on a desk. Since that day I never stepped foot in a regular high school classroom until now, my junior year. By freshman year I was already turning into a drop out. I was into hard core partying and would go for days without coming home. I remember I had a lot of people who actually cared about me, and kept telling me I was a good person who just needed to get help. They were right, but I kept spitting on them, and then finally they just gave up on me and left.

Summer came and I was going to be a sophomore. One day I went to the homies house and I told him that I had $20 and that we should get some beer and bud. He said, "Nah, but let's get some crystal meth." At first I was like "f**k no! I'll never do that Sh*t." But he kept telling me how good it was and that it wasn't that bad. So finally I gave in and we had the crystal delivered to us. When he handed it to me it I didn't even know what I was supposed to do with it. All it looked like was a bunch of white rocks. I asked him if this was what it was supposed to look like, and he said, "Yea." Then he pulled out a pipe that I had never seen before. He put the rocks inside it and he said, "Watch this." He put a lighter underneath the pipe and lit it. It took about four seconds and it started smoking and I saw the rocks melt into a liquid. My homie put the pipe in front of me and said, "Inhale when I tell you to." So he told me to, and I started inhaling it. He told me to breathe out like I was warming my hands up and when I did, so much smoke came out…it was like, damn. When we were done smoking I didn't even feel lit at all, but friend was like "Hell yea you are."

About a month later I was getting high a lot and I overdosed on spice, pills, alcohol and weed. I had to go to the hospital and from there they told me I needed to go to rehab. A week later I was on my way to a treatment center. I stayed there for a month and then got kicked out because I got caught smoking spice. I lasted about two days at home before I was back out on the streets doing drugs again. A month later I got busted and was charged with a felony and sent to a camp for boys. I was there for nine months and now I'm here. It's my junior year in high school and I'm trying to stay out of trouble.

31. <u>Recovering Friends / Family / God</u>

In elementary school my home life wasn't the best. My parents are not together, and in those days, my brother and I were forced to spend every other weekend with our father. He had abandoned us as babies and now was back demanding custody so he wouldn't have to pay child support. We both dreaded going to our father's house because of the way he treated us. As the years went on the abuse was getting worse, but one day my older brother got the nerve to stand up for us and told my mom what was going on at our father's house. As of now I haven't been with my dad since the courts said it was our choice to see him. The only down side was that my brother and I had to see a family counselor for a year.

Throughout middle school I didn't really hangout with bad influences until the end of eighth grade. I got involved with the wrong group of people and went down the same path as them. Even though I was with bad kids, my mom didn't find out and she showed me nothing but love. Over all, my home life was fine, but I couldn't tell my mom what I was doing, so I was constantly lying to her. Once I got into high school I went to a different school than all my friends. To make new friends I started to play football and that got my life back on track. Unfortunately, by my sophomore year I started partying again and hanging out with a bad group of kids. I got pulled up to varsity as a sophomore, but missed some games because of how my life was going. Eventually I quit football so I could spend more time with my party friends. My grades got terrible, and so did my reputation.

My junior year was even worse. I continued down the wrong path until the summer going into my senior year. I was really into hard drugs and partying and was hiding what I was doing from my girlfriend, and everyone else. My motivation for doing anything good was gone and I pretty much hit rock bottom. I messed up my relationship with my mom, my girlfriend, my brother and my closest friends, even with God, all because of drugs and partying.

Losing my girlfriend was like hitting a wall of realization. I finally realized I needed to get my life back together in order to graduate. I started going to a Bible study with kids from school and I got my girlfriend back into my life. She's been my motivation to keep going down the right path. I am going to be sober for life and to graduate from high school. As of now I have an amazing home life, a great relationship with God and I'm doing all of my homework so far.

It feels good to be able to say that I finished my homework and to see how proud my mom and girlfriend are of me. There is no drug that can compare to the feeling of being loved and having the sense of accomplishment that I have. I've had to sacrifice some friends along the way, but it has been worth it to gain the friends I have now who are keeping me on the path to a better life. I'm so thankful for everything I have and I'm never looking back on the past or getting off the path that I'm on now. I'm excited to see how my senior year goes and how the rest of my life is going to turn out.

32. <u>Feeling Stupid</u>

During my seventh grade year things started going very badly. My dad had cheated on my step mom with a woman who is now his girlfriend. There was a lot of fighting and yelling in the house, so it made it difficult to do homework. Eventually my step mom moved out and the girlfriend moved in. I hated that. I got very depressed and started not eating because I was too upset to feel hungry. I can't remember how much I weighed before that but I know I was down to 90lbs. I struggled most of my eighth grade year because I was too distracted with my dad's new girlfriend and her daughter. This new step "sister" and I fought non-stop and this made me angrier every day. I was often too upset to even think about doing homework. Soon I was failing every class and hanging out with other girls who also did poorly in school. I started to think I was just stupid when it came to school. It never occurred to me that any of my academic problems had anything to do with the problems at home.

Junior high faded into high school and I still struggled with feelings that I was not smart enough to do a lot of the work on my own, but I was too embarrassed to get help from anyone. I was afraid they would quit on me. In all of this I got really depressed. When my junior year rolled around I failed all of my classes. My dad stopped being proud of me. He didn't know what to do with me and my school problems so he just gave up on me. I'm now a senior and I want to prove my dad wrong, that I am going to graduate and become something.

33. <u>Where Did My Daddy Go?</u>

During my elementary years my home life starting getting bad. My mom and dad fought all the time, almost every night. I remember one night my dad came home late with make-up all over his shirt and glitter on his face. That night was the worst. I remember mommy crying and both of them yelling back and forth. Shoving me out of the way, my dad hit my mom, so my mom locked me and her in a room. It was hard trying to sleep after everything that had happened. We heard a lot of noises going on in the kitchen. My dad was yelling, so we ran out of the room and we saw my dad covered in blood with pieces of his skin in the sink. He had sliced and cut up all his arms. I remember crying and wondering why he did what he did. I guess I was too young to understand.

When I was about nine my dad left us. He just left without us knowing where, or why. For seven years my dad was not in my life. Ever since he left I felt so empty, especially because he didn't seem to think I was his daughter. I cried every day to myself, hoping my dad would come back, or that I would hear what happened to him.

I loved my dad.

I was daddy's little girl. I thought our bond seemed unbreakable, but I was wrong. I was so devastated thinking he could abandon his children the way he did. He hurt us all, not just my mom or my brother, but especially me. I also remember the day my mom told me it was my fault he left. Tears come down my eyes typing this. I guess she felt as if she was the blame for it, but didn't want to feel that way, so she blamed me. A couple of years went by after dad left and finally my mom met a new guy. I hated him, or maybe I just hated the fact he wasn't my dad. I just couldn't picture my mom with anyone else, but I had to deal with it. Eventually we ended up moving in with this guy.

By my freshman year I still had no contact with my dad. By this time my mom had divorced him. Even though my dad wasn't around, it still hurt. My mom's boyfriend ended up becoming my step dad, and after living with him for several years, I learned to love him. After all, he did step in and support my brother and me as his own children. Looking back, my whole life pretty much revolved around the situation with my dad.

One day toward the end of my sophomore year I arrived home, and my mom was sitting at the kitchen table. Suddenly the phone rang and I ran to answer it. Apparently it was my dad's mom. She said to me,

"Don't hang up, ok. Someone wants to talk to you."

It seemed very strange to me, but I said, "Ok."

Then I heard a man say, "Hello."

I said, "Um, yes. Who is it?"

He replied, "It's me baby, your daddy."

I was so shocked I couldn't believe it. So many thoughts and memories ran through my head I didn't know what to say to him. I had so many questions. Where? Why? How could he do this to me? I couldn't think, so I started to cry. I just handed the phone to my mom, telling her it was my dad. She was also shocked. I ran to my mom, just crying and thinking:

"Where was he for seven whole years?"

It was so sad that I couldn't even talk to him because he just seemed like a complete stranger to me. I didn't know who he was anymore. The saddest part was that my little brother didn't know him at all.

I have since learned that my dad went through a lot himself. He was homeless for a while, caught up in fighting with guys in the streets and spent some time in several hospitals.

Somewhere along the line he became a changed person and has been involved in a Christian ministry in Los Angeles. I'm glad he is ok now and is doing well, but I will never forget the horrible things he did. Our bond will never be the same as it was when I was young. I'm now a junior in high school and I still keep in contact with him. We are ok now, but, like I said, it will never be the same.

I honestly don't know why I'm in this class, but I'm glad that I am. Maybe it's because I did horrible in school last year. I don't know, but I like it. This is the first time I have actually written the real deal for a teacher; it's kind of strange. Maybe it will help me let all this out. I only have one best friend and she is the only other person who knows everything about me.

34. <u>Abandoned</u>

I was in middle school when I discovered why my dad didn't want to move our family to the state where he was working all the time. His job required him to be gone for weeks at a time, so the plan was to move us closer to his job. We even had the house packed up for the move, but he called it off. One day, during a stretch where he was home, our dog got out. My mom and I took my dad's truck and went looking for her in the field behind our house. While I was sitting in the truck I found a phone. I had never seen this phone before so I turned it on and saw a picture of my dad kissing a woman I didn't recognize. I set down the phone, got out of the truck and started running. In a while I saw my dad coming toward the field, probably because he realized he had left his phone in the truck. He yelled my name, but I kept running. I remember wanting to just run forever. Later I came home because I was worried about my mom. As soon as I got near the front yard I saw my dad was sitting on a rock waiting. He had taken the phone from my mom and smashed it. He had me sit down next to him and he told me she was just a friend. I didn't know what to believe. I knew what I saw, but I was so young, and he was my dad...the man I had looked up to my entire life. My mom tried to make things work with my dad for a while. I realize now, she did it for me and my sister.

During these middle school years, my dad was gone most of the time and by eighth grade my mom had filed for divorce. There is a lot more to the story, but I'd be writing this for days if I tried to explain it all. Basically, my dad abandoned his family for another woman. One of the hardest things for me was finding out that he was "fathering" her children; taking them to amusement parks and on family trips. It was like my dad had a whole other life.

It's been hard going to high school without a dad in my life. When I still played sports it was really hard on me when I'd see all the other dads come to watch their sons play. Luckily, I had my mom and sister rooting for me at every game. There is much more to say, but I don't know how to put it in words. My story is still being written every day.

35. <u>Molested / Broken Home / Forced to Move</u>

When I was young my uncle lived with our family and whenever my parents were gone he would touch me and do other stuff. Eventually he left and went to Mexico, and that's when I opened up to my baby sitter and told her what had happened. She then told my mom, and afterwards, my mom told my dad. I remember going to the police station very scared and nervous and some cops were talking to me. In the back were my parents crying: it was actually the first time I had ever seen my dad cry. After they talked to me they told me to wait outside because they were going to talk to my parents. While I was sitting down a cop lady came and gave me a stuffed animal. It was a kitty, and till this very day, I still have it.

A few months went by and my parents got a divorce because my dad cheated on my mom. Now I have two half-sisters and a brother. To make things worse, my mom got married again and I hate my stepdad because he made me move to this town. I have absolutely no family here and I hate it. No matter how many times I would complain my mom would not let me move back with my dad. The first day of school here I felt like a loner. I missed all my friends.

36. <u>No One to Kick My A**</u>

I started struggling in school my sophomore year. It's disappointing, because I can never get that back. The reason I had an academic downfall was because my mom and stepdad got divorced. My mom and stepdad got together when I was one-and-a-half. My real dad was a major alcoholic and took pills. He died in January of 2007. That was upsetting, but didn't hurt me academically, not like when my mom and stepdad got divorced. They got divorced just this last year, but it was for the best. Whenever I did something that upset him or ticked him off—just little things, like, if something of my chores wasn't perfect, or I smirked, or said something that he didn't like—he would beat my ass.

I remember one time he pushed me to the floor. Then he told me to get up, and as I was getting up, he kicked me in the face to knock me back down. I remember another time he was choking me and was telling me to answer him, but I couldn't because I couldn't breathe. Anyhow, I could go on and on, but that's not the point. So my mom and my stepdad got divorced, and it made my life a lot easier. I really didn't have to care about school that much anymore because my mom wasn't going to beat my ass if I messed up. If I had to say what the roots were that got me off track in school, I'd say they were divorce, focusing on fun (not school), depression, laziness, violence at home, stress, abuse, feeling like a failure (my stepdad would call me a stupid piece of shit all the time) and shame/fear/regret. But to be honest, I really don't mind that he did those things to me, but when he would start going off on my mom, that hurt way more. So when my mom finally left him I had so much freedom. It was like a weight had been lifted off my body. I just stopped caring about school because there wasn't anyone to kick my ass anymore.

Now I'm in my junior year and I feel like I'm on top of the world; I feel that I can accomplish anything. I messed up for a whole year. Now it's time to bring it back around. I'm going to try with all my heart to do my best. Last year I think I had a 2.0 or less—I'm not sure. I'm determined not to be just an average student, but to be at the top of my class and to put forth all my effort. I am determined to get a 4.0, no matter what obstacles I encounter. I've always wanted to be a pilot. I know I won't be if I keep this nonsense up. I am absolutely 100% on board to change my life back around. It's time to get to work!

37. <u>Please don't fight with mommy tonight.</u>

When I was little my father used to beat my mom and me. I'm believe my father resented me, he wouldn't even take care of me unless my mom paid him. One night we were all eating and my brother had just gone to bed. My parents told me to go to sleep, also. So I said goodnight to my dad and whispered in his ear, "Please try not to fight with Mom tonight." The next thing I knew he smacked me in the face and threw his dinner onto the floor. My mom came in and tried to help, but she only got the back of his hand, too. It was like that with my parents, they always fought. My dad was an alcoholic and he was never proud of anything. He finally left us after I called the cops on him when I was seven. That night is something that I don't want to relive.

One thing I never got to do growing up was go to a daddy-daughter dance, or banquet. I hide behind a smile a lot, but I have a lot of baggage I need to get rid of. My dad now lives in another town and I haven't visited him in a year. I hear he is sober, but I'm scared to see him.

Last time I saw him he did things that made me not want to go near him ever again.

Made in the USA
San Bernardino, CA
10 July 2016